Nature Stories with a Twist

Iris Gray Dowling

Faithful Life Publishers
North Fort Myers, FL

FaithfulLifePublishers.com

Nature Stories with a Twist
ISBN: 978-1-937129-68-2

Copyright: © 2013 Iris Gray Dowling

www.irisgraydowling.com
irisgdow@juno.com

Published and printed by:
Faithful Life Publishers
3335 Galaxy Way
North Fort Myers, FL 33903

888.720.0950

www.FaithfulLifePublishers.com
info@FaithfulLifePublishers.com

Acknowledgements: Elsie Shepherd and Hazel Duncan, reading editors. Cleo Swymer for jellyfish and sparrow sketches. John Dowling arranged travel explorations.

All Rights Reserved. No part of this publication may be reproduced, stored in a Retrieval system, or transmitted in any form or by any means—electronic, mechanical, digital, photocopy, recording, or any other—except for brief quotations in printed reviews, without the prior permission of the author and publisher.

Printed in the United States of America

18 17 16 15 14 13   1 2 3 4 5

Preface

This book contains over 35 Nature Stories telling about objects of God's Creation. A few science facts are given but much can be added by doing more scientific investigation.

Jesus, the Master Teacher, taught lessons from nature. He demonstrated spiritual truths by using the people's environment. This author has also endeavored to use nature stories by taking interesting facts from nature and turning them into memorable lessons that make a spiritual point.

The author is aware that children learn when they are involved, so she included some activities with a few of the stories to get children interested and involved. It is exciting to watch when children start doing additional research and start making their own applications from nature.

It is the author's desire that all those who read these stories will increase their faith in God and His eternal plan.

This book is a gift from the author —

Iris Gray Dowling

Philippians 4:13

Table of Contents

The Creator Made Lots of Space 7
    Be a Steady Shining Light (Stars) 10
    The Sun's Effects on Us 11
    Planets: Is There Life on the Planets? 13
    The Lesser Light—The Moon 16
    Did God Create a Heaven and a Hell? 18
    Why Didn't Columbus Believe the Earth was Flat? 19
God Made Some for a Higher Place (wild and domesticated sheep) . 20
Asking for Wisdom (chimps) 23
Follow the Right Scent (hounds) 25
The Seeing-Eye of the Blind 25
Man's Best Friend? (dogs) 27
The Family Unit (wolves) 31
The Rewards of Making Wise Choices (coyotes) 33
Where is Your Treasure Stored (squirrels) 35
The Groundhog's Predictions 37
A Smelly Defense (skunks) 39
The Donkey Made a Difference 41
The Faithful Horse 44
Seeking Whom He May Devour (lion) 45
A Life in Darkness (moles) 47
Earthworms Need Air 49
Who Do We Imitate? (catbird or mockingbird) 51
Important to God (sparrows) 53
Does a Praying Mantis Really Pray or Prey? 55
Can you Smell that Stink Bug? 57
An Insect that is Not Lazy! (ant) 60
Bee a Faithful Worker 62
Thankful for Fleas? 64
Getting Your Attention (flies, lice, locusts) 66
A Special Touch—How to make a butterfly and moth collection 69
How the Tadpole Changes (frogs and toads) 76
The Stinging Beauty (jellyfish) 79
The Spider's Parlor 82
Hold on to God's Truth (Venus's-Flytrap) 85
The Tent—A Temporary Home 87
Puzzle Answers 91
Challenges from the Author 93

The Creator Made Lots of Space

The Solar System is made up of the sun, planets, their moons, and other smaller objects such as asteroids, meteors, and comets. The sun is the center of our solar system; however, there are billions of other stars that are trillions of miles apart and trillions of miles farther into space. There are some we can't see from earth. Wow! Such vastness in space isn't possible to imagine for most human minds. (See Endnote #1, pg. 9)

The sun, a tiny star by space measurements, is closest to the earth—about 93 million miles away. The sun is twenty-five trillion, sixty-three billion miles from the next closest star. To show the sun's size in comparison, one star in Orion, named Betelgeuse, is about 400 times the sun's diameter.

God, the creator, put all these trillions of enormous stars in their positions. They move at extremely fast speeds. They stay within the path God designed. This shows the supernatural creator—God—and His omnipotent power. He holds each heavenly object where he put it and has kept it there for thousands of years. No one object will stray from its assigned position until God commands the change.

In light of these facts, if I didn't believe in God, I'd have to recognize that He created everything in space. Anyone who studies Astronomy has to admit a supernatural power is in charge of this vast, complex universe.

In 1968 Apollo 8 carried three astronauts into space: Frank Borman, Jim Lovell, and William Anders. They orbited the moon ten times. On the ninth time they skimmed 68 miles above the gray, bleak surface of the moon. Lovell described the beauty of earth and commented on the colorlessness of the moon and the extreme loneliness of space, so far from earth. Borman's photograph of the earth hanging above the moon's horizon, is considered the most famous shot ever taken in space. It was put on a postage stamp.

Knowing the three would be circling the earth on Christmas Eve, 1968, and that they would be expected to send a message back to earth, they carried Genesis 1:1-10, from the *King James Version*, typed on fireproof paper. The chosen readings proved extremely appropriate for how they felt and what they had observed.

Bill Anders read verses 1 to 4: "*In the beginning God created the heaven and the earth. And the earth was without form, and void; and darkness was upon the face of the deep. And the Spirit of God moved upon the face of the waters. And God said, 'Let there be light:' and there was light. And God saw the light, that it was good: and God divided the light from the darkness.*"

Jim Lovell continued with verses 5-8: "*And God called the light Day, and the darkness he called Night. And the evening and the morning were the first day. And God said, 'Let there be a firmament in the midst of the waters, and let it divide the waters from the waters.' And God made the firmament, and divided the waters which were under the firmament from the waters which were above the firmament: and it was so. And God called the firmament Heaven. And the evening and the morning were the second day.*"

Frank Borman finished with verse 9, 10: "*And God said, 'Let the waters under the heaven be gathered together unto one place, and let the dry land appear': and it was so. And God called the dry land Earth, and the gathering together of the waters he called Seas: and God saw that it was good.*"

Endnote #1

Stars and their distance from the Earth

No one knows the actual number of stars. Scientists know there are many galaxies like our Milky Way Galaxy which contains our sun, planets and about 200,000,000,000 stars (suns). When we speak of the distance of the stars, we measure distance in *light-years*.

A *light-year* means how long it takes light to travel from the distances in space.

(To translate *light-years* into miles, multiply the number of *light-years* by 6 million-million miles.)

Rather difficult—right?

Here are a few stars and their distance from the Earth. Many stars have not been named.

    Sun .. ..about 93 million miles
    Polaris . . .. 190 light-years distant
    Betelgeuse. .. .. 192 light-years distant
    Rigel. .. .. 543 light-years distant
    Pegasus .. .. 441 light-years distant
    Sirius .. .. 48.3 light-years distant

Be a Steady Shining Light
(The stars)

There are billions of stars we can't see—more than the sands of the shore. There are only thousands we can see with our human eyes. Stars are ball-shaped suns, which don't have points. They provide their own light and heat from the burning gases. Their heat temperature is measured in thousands of degrees. They are so far away from earth that we measure distance by hundreds of thousands of light years.

Our human minds can't comprehend the vast amount of space God created in heaven's universe. Stars are trillions of miles apart. God made stars stay in their courses by a gravitational attraction between them. Nothing happened by accident or how else can one explain why these millions of huge objects don't crash into each other.

Stars are always shining with a steady light. They appear to twinkle, but don't. In the great distance between us, the air moves to cause the twinkling effect and also gives the star a point effect.

The closest star is our sun. It is 93 million miles from earth. Other stars can't be seen from earth in the day because this closer star, our sun, gives off a closer brighter light that blocks out the fainter distant lights of other stars. The earth moves on its axis turning our side away from the sun. Then we can see the stars at night.

As Christians, we need to be steady lights, like stars shining brightly for Jesus, so others can see His light shining through us. We shouldn't let anything block out God's light or make it fainter. It should shine day and night like stars do.

(Biblio: *Q & A Book of Nature*, '64)
(Iris's story "Be A Steady Shining Light" first published by Shining Star Magazine, 2001

The Sun's Effects on Us

There are trillions of stars we can't see and only thousands we can see with our eyes. The closest and smallest star is our sun—about 93 million miles from earth. All stars, including the sun, are shining balls consisting of hot gases like hydrogen, helium, calcium, iron, etc.

The sun has major effects on planet earth. Without it the earth would probably not exist. The sun's gravitational pull causes earth to move in an oval path around the sun, not spin out into space. The gravitational pull of the sun and moon causes ocean tides.

Without sunlight there would be no living things on earth. There would be coldness worse than man has ever felt or been able to produce. Light and heat rays from the sun make a difference between everything on earth being cold, dark, and dead, or warm, light, and growing. The sun surrounds the earth with a fiery ocean of gases important to our survival. The wrong combination of gases would kill people and animals quickly.

Without the sun there would be no air, wind, or weather changes. The sun lifts water from earth into the air to make rain, which supplies all growing things on earth with one of the most needed elements. (The Water Cycle)

The sun helps plants manufacture their own food. This food helps people and animals live and grow by providing energy from stored sunlight. Only small amounts of the vast reserves of solar energy reach the earth, but they perform miracles on this planet.

In areas of the world where there is less sunlight, people get irritable and depressed in the dark winter season and look forward to the appearance of light. (SAD=Seasonal Affective Disorder)

God is light and shines on us just as the sun shines its beautiful life-giving light on and into the earth. God shines the light of His glory in our hearts. He wants to shine that glory, the love of Jesus Christ, in and through us to others.

God created the sun to rise early in the morning. We should be anxious to get God's spiritual light early each day to be more useful throughout the day.

Plants need daily sunshine or they experience no growth. It's the same for a believer without God's light—no growth!

Just as the sun's light makes plants fruitful, we need to let God make us fruitful by abiding in His light and letting Him fill us with life and fruitfulness. A life without God's light is dark, cold, and unproductive.

Is there such a thing as light not shining? Not likely. Let's open the shutters and let His light in. His light can only shine in and out of me as much as I let it.

Planets: Is There Life on the Planets?

There are eight planets orbiting our sun; our sun orbits the Milky Way galaxy, which is our family of stars. Those planets are: Mercury, Venus, Earth, Mars, Jupiter, Saturn, Uranus, and Neptune (in order from the sun). Since 2006 Pluto has been considered a dwarf planet because it doesn't fit the scientific criteria for a full planet.

The planets sail around the sun in the original path the creator placed them in. All move in a westward direction. Some take much longer to make one orbit because of the distance from the sun—literally billions of miles.

Planets are dark solid bodies much smaller than the sun or the stars. They get heat and light from the sun. The distance from the sun determines the amount of heat and light received by each planet. Because of the incorrect amount of light, heat, or gases to support life, as we know it, the earth is thought to be the only planet that has the ability to support life.

Mercury, Venus, Mars, Jupiter, Saturn, and Uranus are closest to the sun. They reflect light from the sun and can be seen from earth at night without a telescope.

Many people don't realize the difference between these planets and stars in the night sky. Planets differ in that they shine with a steady light and don't seem to twinkle as stars do.

Planets do not have their own light, but reflect the sun's light. The position of planets shifts slightly eastward each night, while stars stay in the same position.

Planets are dark, solid bodies much smaller than the sun or stars, even though they don't appear that way to earth's observers. All the planets together weigh less than a hundredth of the sun's weight. The sun is the closest and smallest star.

Planets are so far apart that we couldn't travel from one to another in our lifetime with a round-trip ticket. We seem to be extremely small specks in a vast universe of planets, stars, and many other heavenly objects God made.

However, each person is significant to God who created life on planet earth where He provided the right amount of gases and distance from the sun to support life.

To God each person isn't just a speck, but a unique human being who He says in Psalms 139:14-18 is made wonderfully and for His pleasure. He desires fellowship with the people He made. That's why He sent His Son to die and take the guilt and punishment for our sins. When we accept His forgiveness we can enjoy His fellowship. God's greatness and love should cause each person to bow in humble worship and adoration of such a great caring creator.

Endnote #2

<u>Planets</u> in order of their Orbits from the sun, it's <u>distance from the sun</u> (in miles) at its closest and farthest points; and the average <u>day and night temperatures in Fahrenheit degrees</u>.

Planet	Closest Point	Farthest Point	Temperatures Day	Night
Mercury	29,000,000	43,000,000	625 F	80 F
Venus	66,800,000	67,700,000	980 F	620 F
Earth	91,400,000	94,500,000	60 F	40 F
Mars	128,000,000	155,000,000	-10 F	-150 F
Jupiter	460,000,000	507,000,000	-170 F	-170 F
Saturn	838,000,000	937,000,000	-240 F	-240 F
Uranus	1,700,000,000	1,870,000,000	-240 F	?
Neptune	2,771,000,000	2,819,000,000	-280 F	?

(Here is a puzzle to help you remember the names of the planets in order. In the lines below, cross out the first letter and every third letter after it.

Write the 8 planets below:

smelrcpurtyvhenfusseazrtghmkartsjsupeithero

Mercury Venus Earth Mars

saxtuhrndrqansusbnexptfunve

Saturn Uranus Neptune

The Lesser Light—the Moon

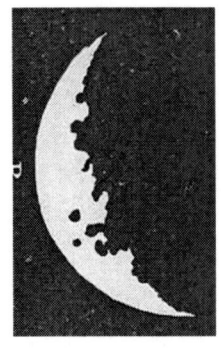

There are many moons in the universe. Some other planets have satellites; for example, Jupiter has twelve moons or satellites. The earth has one moon that we see in the night sky. The moon—Earth's nearest neighbor in space—gives off no light of its own, but reflects (casts back) light from the sun. The moon seems to change its size and shape, but doesn't. We can only see the parts that are lighted by the sun.

The moon travels around the earth every 29 ¼ days. It is about 238,850 miles from earth and it takes about six days for a rocket to get to the moon and back. On July 20, 1969 Neal Armstrong visited the moon and said it was a huge ball of grey rock which reflects the sun's light; a silent, lonely place with a lot of craters where no life was found. Most rocks were of the volcanic type. (When I walked on the volcanic surfaces in Crater National Park, Hawaii, where volcanoes had erupted a few years earlier, I was told it resembled the surface of the moon.)

People say they see a man's face on the moon. Because the moon has no air, no wind, and no water, they only see deep craters which form the eyes seen from earth. Craters were formed by meteoroids (solid objects that travel through space in orbits around the sun) striking its surface because of the moon's lack of atmosphere, unlike what surrounds our earth.

Gravity on the moon is six times weaker than on earth. The moon travels 2300 miles per hour on its revolution around the earth as the earth travels around the sun in its orbit. The moon is not without its effect on the earth and its people such as ocean tides and eclipses.

Boys and girls, you can try this experiment: Get a bike reflector, a flashlight, and a globe. Have one child hold the reflector (moon), another child hold a flashlight (sun), while the third child stands near the reflector holding the globe.(earth or world). Notice the reflector looks dark before a light shines on it. Shine the flashlight on the reflector and watch it light up and cast a glow back on the globe.

People are somewhat like the moon in that they are nothing but blackness without the sunlight of God's love. When we know Jesus as Savior, we can reflect the light of the Sun of Righteousness—Jesus Christ (Malachi 4:2; John 8:12) to people who have never seen it. It's amazing that God shows us through His creation how important it is for Believers to be a good reflector of His light. (Matthew 5:14-16)

Did God Create a Heaven and a Hell?

Jesus said in John 14:2, 3 that He is preparing a place for believers. Some have questioned how there is enough space for the comfort of all believers since Adam. What do you think? After studying the incomprehensible expanse of space, I think God will have no problem preparing a place for all who believe in Him. (Job 22:12)

Neither will He have a problem preparing the new city, Jerusalem, which will be 1500 miles square. That's a gigantic city! (Revelation 21:16, 17).

God's Heaven is thought to be beyond these expanses we know about, but wherever God wants us to dwell forever, He is able to create that place. He has hinted to us that there is enough space for all believers, beyond the part our human minds can comprehend.

The vastness of space makes me think of Jude 13. God is not only preparing a place for believers (John 14:1-3), but He also will prepare a place in outer darkness and loneliness for those who refuse to believe or accept His great salvation gift (Ephesians 2:8,9). This study of space has caused me to wonder about the place of this loneliness and suffering for all eternity.

Astronomers tell us there are more galaxies beyond what we know about. Certainly there is enough space for each person since the beginning of time to dwell in loneliness.

I even wondered about the fire that is never quenched. The millions of gigantic stars are made up of burning gases which burn continually—a fire that never goes out. If you don't believe they can burn a human, think of the sunburn you got from our closest star 93 million miles away. I don't want to feel that burning pain too often, do you? (Luke 16:23)

I once heard the testimony of a man who shook his fist at God in defiance. After a terrible accident he lay unconscious in the emergency room. He told about the awful, unbearable loneliness and thick, black darkness he felt. He couldn't explain how he recovered from death defying injuries except that God let him live to repent and tell you about it. He said "I know I never want to return to such a place again and now I believe there is a God in Heaven who intervenes in the lives of people. (2 Samuel 22:6; Psalms 116:3)

Why Didn't Columbus Believe the Earth was Flat?

When Columbus lived some people thought the earth was flat, but most educated people believed it was round. Columbus, who was self-educated, studied the Holy Bible. He knew God created the earth and had control over everything He made. He found these words in Isaiah 40:22. *"It is He (God) that sitteth upon the circle of the earth."*

Columbus believed if he sailed west he would come to the Far East (India or China). He did not reach India, but proved his theory was true.

Columbus had faith that God would take care of him. After solving many problems he started his journey west on August 3, 1492. He took three ships; the Nina, Pinta, and the Santa Maria. He landed on San Salvador October 12, 1492. Columbus Day is celebrated because he discovered a new part of the world, part of the Americas.

Columbus sailed to other islands of the West Indies. He called the people *Indians* because he thought these islands were part of India. He was named the "Admiral of the Ocean Sea" because of his bravery and many sailing discoveries. Now you understand why we have called the Redmen *Indians* for so many years.

What do we call them now? _Native American_.

"Christopher Columbus sailed the ocean blue in _1792_."
                                                           (year)

God Made Some for A Higher Place

The Bighorn Sheep, Dall Sheep, and Stone Sheep make their homes high in the mountains of western North America. The Bighorn is named because of its large curved horns. Unlike other sheep, these species don't have wool, only hair like a deer.

These sheep are comfortable on the highest ledges and mountain peaks. When pursued by a hunter, wolf, or coyote, they go higher where predators find it hard to follow. These sure-footed sheep dash from cliff to cliff at great speeds. Even young lambs leap from rock to ledge at dangerous heights without fear. Usually the higher they go the safer they become; however, young lambs don't always escape prowling mountain lions or soaring eagles.

When I traveled in the mountains of Alaska and in the Western Rockies of United States and Canada it was a thrill to finally spot a Dall Sheep, high on the ridges, with the help of my strong binoculars.

In Acts 20, a young man went to sleep while listening to Paul preach a long time. He didn't stay sitting on the third story window ledge, but fell to the ground and died. Paul immediately used God's power to raise him from the dead. The young man went back upstairs to listen to God's Word being preached until midnight, then went home with his family. Don't you think his life must have been changed because of what happened that night? How many of us would go to hear God's messenger if we knew he would speak until midnight? God must have had a special plan in mind for that young man.

God wants all Christians to reach spiritual mountain heights by having a daily time with Him. We need to study His Word, talk with Him about our problems, and have fellowship with other Christians. This helps believers grow stronger against Satan's attacks. The devil seeks those he can draw from this higher place with God. Our maturing in Christ and gaining spiritual strength deters Satan from gaining victories in our lives. How pleased God is when we prepare and accept victory provided by His Son.

(This story by Iris was First published in *Kids Ministry Ideas.*)
Bibliography: *Marvels & Mysteries of Our Animal World,* Reader's Digest Assn. p.93.
World Book Encyclopedia "Bighorn & Mountain Sheep".

Domesticated Sheep

At one stage in my rural life I lived on a sheep farm. Domesticated sheep are not as wise as the wild sheep. They will wander off and not be able to find their way home. The farmer has to search for them before a dog or predator catches them. Domesticated dogs could run a sheep until the sheep drops from exhaustion. The farmer puts extra strands of wire or blocked wire along the ground to keep the sheep from crawling out of the pasture. Still, big dogs sometimes jump into the fields and kill the sheep.

Sheep shearing is an important time each spring. The weight and thickness of the sheep's wool may cause him to become overheated and die of exhaustion or roll over on his back and not be able to roll back to get on his feet—somewhat like a turtle that is turned over on his shell. I've seen sheep that died on their backs, after struggling to get up.

The shearers are quite skilled by usually cutting the wool off the sheep in one large piece without cutting its body. How funny the sheep looks when he is first shorn, and how comfortable he feels, especially if warm days arrive early in the spring.

The Bible gives many examples of people being like sheep. They wander away from God, their shepherd, and get into all kinds of dangers and troubles before being found by the Shepherd. (Isaiah 53:6; Psalms 119:176a)

A beautiful illustration is that of the Shepherd giving his life for his sheep (John10:11). He endures great danger until he finds that one lamb that is lost. It is always the Shepherd's desire to gather every lost sheep into the safety of the fold, even if he has to carry it home. What a beautiful picture of the Good Shepherd (Jesus) rescuing the lost person from the fields of sin. Jesus gave his life for each and every lost sheep, even me.

Another beautiful picture shows the gentle shepherd watching the sheep as they contentedly enjoy the green pastures beside the still waters as seen in Psalms 23:1, 2. What a comfort to the Christian who abides in the Savior's love!

Puzzle Question: Can you name three chapters in the Bible that talk about sheep and the shepherd? Two are in the Old Testament and one is in the New Testament.

Isaiah 40:11 is like the New Testament chapter. Look at Isaiah 40:11 and fill in the blanks: "*He (Jesus) shall feed his flock like a _____: He shall gather the _____ (baby sheep) with His arm and carry them in His bosom (close to His heart), and shall gently lead those that are with young.*"

22

Asking For Wisdom

In 1999 a chimpanzee operated electrical instruments to guide a spacecraft. How could an animal have enough brains to do that?

Scientists believe chimps are the most intelligent and cleverest of all animals. They learn faster and can be trained to operate machines. However, chimps can't think of a plan, write it down, and carry it out.

Chimpanzee

God created chimps to swing in the trees of the rain forest. While on the ground they crawl on all fours. Their forefeet are similar to human hands with shorter thumbs. Although a full-grown chimp is the size of a man, its intelligence isn't equal. It is very clever and can imitate easily. Its ability to do tricks isn't a sign of intelligence, but of training and imitation. Adult chimps can solve some complicated problems.

Even though chimps can be trained to manipulate the complicated instruments of a spacecraft, they can't build it. Chimps can't reason or figure out complicated math problems. They can't choose a course of action and complete it; however, God created people with brains for thinking and reasoning.

A chimp lacks spiritual thinking. It doesn't have the knowledge of good and evil. It doesn't have a soul and can't choose its eternal destiny. Humans, on the other hand, can recognize there is a God. They know good and evil. God gave varying amounts of intelligence to humans and wants them to recognize His unlimited wisdom and power. We're told in God's Word to ask for more wisdom. If we ask with believing faith He'll grant our request. Try it and see.

God's creation of people was different from chimps or any other animals. A chimp doesn't realize there is a God who made it. All animals are unable to ask for more wisdom as people can.

God told a great man in the Bible to ask for anything he wanted and God would give it. (I Kings 3:5, 9-12)

Who was this man? _Solomon_

What did he ask for? _wisdom_

Was God pleased with his wish? _Yes_

Did God give him what he wished for? _Yes_

(First written by Iris and published in *Partners SS Papers*. 5.2001)

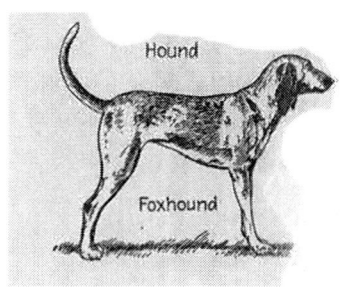

Follow the Right Scent
(Thoughts for the New Year)

"Sniff, Sniff!" That dog never watches where he's going. He just keeps his nose to the ground. "Wuff, Wuff!" That's the sound a hound dog makes when it catches the scent. Hounds, a breed of tracking dogs, have a keen sense of smell, endurance, and a natural intelligence with a desire to please their masters. During obedience training each dog learns to follow different scents. A good hound can detect a scent from tracks or bushes that a body has brushed against. This breed of dog can follow a scent several hours old if it hasn't been disturbed by rain or mixed with other smells. Hounds have proved useful in tracking criminals or lost people.

The correct path for the Christian to follow this New Year is clearly shown in God's Word. Like a hound, we should learn obedience, endurance, and the desire to please our master. God wants us to listen carefully, obey wise counsel, and apply the Biblical principles in our lives. While we're thinking about making New Year's resolutions and trying to keep our thoughts focused on God's path, we need to remember, wrong influences and unbelieving friends can steal our attention away from God. Freedom of choice is a gift from God; however, He allows us to choose our path and our friends, but he desires for us to keep our life centered on Him.

The Seeing-Eye of the Blind

It takes an especially trained dog to become the eyes for the blind. The dog must be submissive and obedient, yet independent enough to decide when the blind master needs help or protection.

During the early years of life a dog goes through several training periods with a seeing master. Some dogs don't make it to training school because their size and personality aren't adequate. Others don't get to training school because they don't pass the temperament, obedience, and alertness phase. They may not be appropriate for a seeing-eye dog.

When a dog passes all the training and tests successfully, it is ready to do the important job of serving a blind master. A dog and an anxious master are carefully matched since the dog will provide sight for a person not able to see. A seeing-eye dog is a light in the darkness.

We, as Christians, are to be God's lights in a dark world. We are to do the job of showing others the path to heaven and to a better life while living on earth. In order to be God's lights every day, we must have those qualities of obedience, submissiveness, dependability, and daily renewal recommended in God's training manual. Being obedient to our training manual—God's Word—will make us better lights for God in whatever paths of life He may place us.

For more information about helping to train seeing-eye dogs look for the "guide dog" heading in any encyclopedia and contact the Seeing-Eye Dog Training Center.

(First written by Iris and published in *Kids' Ministry Ideas*, 4.2000.)

Man's Best Friend?
(Based on a true event)

The soiled fleecy doll looked like our dog pulled it out of the neighbor's trash, but she didn't. Tippy, a thirty-five pound mutt, loved her doll so much it reminded me of the "old horse" in the story of *The Velveteen Rabbit*. It literally showed the signs of endearing love.

Do dogs think about love? In my mind, dogs do a lot of thinking. They think about being near their masters, and aren't happy being alone. They also think about protecting those they love. They think about favorite toys, people, smells, and food.

Tippy, had one favorite doll. After the past five years of her loving treatment the doll showed signs of her devoted attention. Its dingy look came from being tossed around in the garage, or the barn, or anywhere she happened to be. A new clean doll had no appeal, just like a child who carries his old worn blankie and doesn't want a new one.

Tippy loved to squeeze the doll and make it squeak. Her eyes sparkled with joy when her master tossed it. She never tired of the game of retrieving the doll and carrying it back to have it tossed over and over again.

One night as I walked to the barn to feed and water the horses and ponies Tippy went along carrying her dolly in her mouth. One side of the barn, piled high with hay bales, provided a neat play area. Tippy jumped up on the bales near the roof where she waited for me to finish the barn chores. She played with her doll—tossing it around and making it squeak like a cat playing with a mouse.

I continued to feed the animals and freshen their stalls until all the chores were done. I called Tippy to come and escort me back to the house. She wouldn't come. After several calls with no response I knew she must have a reason for disobeying, so I went up on the bales to check. She stared at me, but would not move from her spot. At that moment I remembered her doll. That would make her come.

"Where's your doll, Tippy?" I asked. She didn't move from her perch in the hay mow, but her eyes followed me as I searched the stalls, feed boxes, corners, and hay mow. Her doll was no where to be found.

"What did you do with your doll?" I asked. She bounced her head up and down and flashed her sparkling eyes, but didn't budge from her spot. I looked around the hay mow again. I pushed a few of the top bales over, but still didn't see her cherished doll.

"It's late, Tippy. We have to go." I tugged on her collar and she reluctantly came down with me. "I'll look more for your doll tomorrow," I said. Her lagging pace going to the house gave evidence that her thoughts were back at the barn. I thought she'd forget about it once we got to the house, but all night and the next day Tippy showed no interest in any other activity. She barely touched her breakfast. Mostly I noticed her lying by the door. I assumed she was waiting for me to go to the barn for chores.

Finally, when I said, "Let's go feed the horses," Tippy leaped from her spot and pranced to the door with a change in her step. She got to the barn far ahead of me and paused anxiously for the door to be opened.

With just a small space Tippy squeezed in and bounded up to the hay mow, to the very place I found her resting the night before. Until I finished feeding the horses, she stayed in that spot as if she had been assigned guard duty.

When I was ready to leave the barn she acted the same way as the night before—perched on the same bale. Her eyes revealed determination not to leave that spot.

Finally, I thought Tippy must know something I don't. Her doll was still missing. Did she know where it was? I thought maybe she did, so I lifted the bales from that spot, going down to a depth of five feet. There, I found her doll. It had fallen deep in the spaces between the bales. Amazingly, she knew it was down there, but couldn't move those monstrous bales to get it.

Upon seeing her beloved dolly she danced up and down and gripped the dolly in her mouth with a sparkling glitter in her eyes. She pranced directly to the door ready to escort me to the house. As we walked I could see how she happily carried her dolly with a different gate than she used the night before.

Once we got to the house she ran to her bed and slept with her dolly between her front legs all night. It was almost like she thought, *I brought you home. I never want to lose you again.* The way Tippy focused on finding her lost doll reminds me of the story of the "Lost Sheep" in Luke 15:3-7. The shepherd searched and searched for his lost sheep until he found it. There was no quitting until the lost one was brought home. Jesus, the Good Shepherd, is still looking for each one so He can take them to His heavenly home.

(I think Tippy's story shows an amazing feat of focused memory lasting over a period of more than twenty-four hours when other events could have caused distractions for a dog).

Dogs not only remember their toys, but unselfishly remember the desires of their masters. They often choose to please the master before themselves. It is amazing that God made so many different kinds of dogs for different reasons and uses. He created dogs in many sizes, colors, looks, and talents to suit the needs of different people. Some dogs are companions, farm workers, rescuers, drug sniffers, guides for the blind and deaf, and much more. In the last few years dogs have been trained to aid masters who are seizure prone. Many times dogs have awakened their masters when their house was on fire or some other danger was lurking. If dogs didn't have an unusual kind of thinking ability and love in caring for their masters, many more lives would have been lost. It's no wonder the dog is called, "Man's Best Friend!"

Puzzle Question: Fill in the blanks by looking in your Bible at Proverbs 18:24. Find Proverbs after Psalms (middle book of the Bible). "A man (person) that has _friends_ must show himself friendly: and there is a _friend_ that sticks closer than a brother."

Do you know a friend like that? _Yes_

The Family Unit

Gray Wolf

A **wolf** is a wild animal resembling a large German shepherd dog. It has longer legs and larger feet, which help it to run for hours at a speed of 20 miles per hour.

Wolves can be white, red, or gray depending on their natural habitat. They have strong family ties. The male and female mate and often stay together for life. The babies are born in a den each spring. Both parents provide the food and train the pups. However, the young wolves don't leave the family, but travel in packs, or family units. When they get separated, they howl, which helps them find and get back to the family group.

In the Far Northern areas wolves still live close to the purpose God intended for them. They hunt sick and injured deer, moose, and caribou, which make for a stronger herd. This helps to prevent overpopulation of grass-eating animals in areas with sparse food supply.

The wolves' devotion to the family could be an example for Christians. In God's plan two people are to marry for life and raise their family together. Both are to help train the children. Whenever someone in the family has a need, all should ban together to help.

When one member of God's family has a need or is feeling lonely, other members should rally around him with prayer, encouragement and deeds of kindness to sustain him through the problem time. This is part of God's perfect plan.

(First written by Iris and published in *Partners SS Papers*, Christian Light Pub., 5.2002.)

Puzzle Activity: Look in the Word Search below and find these 12 words from the story. Then write down the letters not used in the puzzle. Cross out all but one of the X's and you will find a new title and fact for the story.

HOWL	FAMILY	PUPS
DEER	WOLVES	MOOSE
WILD	PACKS	NORTH
DEVOTION	CARIBOU	FAR

```
X A N X F A M I L Y X X E
X A P U P S M P A C K S P
L E X X W I L D X A F R O
M X N X O N A T U R E X X
X H O W L T M H E I E X X
F A R X V X O W O B L E F
X H T D E V O T I O N A D
S X H A S X S X F U A M I
L Y X I N X E X D E N S X
```

__ _____ ____ _____

___ ____ ___ _

_____ __ ___

The Rewards of Making Wise Choices

The **coyote,** a member of the dog/wolf family, is thought to be wise, clever, and intelligent. It resembles a German Shepherd dog, but is no taller than twenty inches and weighs about thirty pounds.

Coyotes are known for their long sad howls heard in the night. They seem to have a communication system which tells of triumph or warning.

The coyote uses its wits for survival where food supplies are sparse. They stalk smaller animals and steal their prey. Mr. Coyote tangles with most animals for food, but for some reason stays away from the Mountain Lion.

Coyotes catch insects, rodents, rabbits, squirrels, gophers, and even eat dead animals killed on the highway. They also like chickens, lambs, or small calves which causes angered farmers to hunt them, ignoring the good coyotes do in destroying insects and rodents that deplete grass crops.

God made coyotes able to find food by using cleverness and bravery in capturing it, as well as to escape human detection. The wise coyote trips the traps and robs the bait. Coyotes show wise actions in escaping tracking dogs by leaving them running in circles, or losing the trail when Mr. Coyote goes up stream or hops on the back of a truck. He can escape by running as fast as forty miles per hour.

In Genesis 14, Lot had been living in an evil place. He had to be rescued from evil people by Abram and his men, but Lot decided to go back to that evil city and live among sinful people again. We wonder where his wisdom was in making such a decision. Perhaps he wasn't in as close fellowship with God as he should have been and Satan's lures attracted him. Sad to say, he didn't go alone. He took his family with him.

Several times Abram asked God not to destroy the cities where Lot was living if God could find ten righteous people there. God could not find even ten in those wicked cities of Sodom and Gomorrah, but He rescued Lot's family as a favor to his servant, Abram. Lot and his family didn't seem too happy about being rescued though. Lot's wife looked back when she was told not to.

God gave us the story of Lot as an example of someone who made poor choices. He gives us wisdom and free choices. He gave us His word as a guide in making good choices.

God doesn't want us just to say we belong to Him, but live our lives making choices that show it. He wants us to actually live our lives making choices to please Him as Abram did. God blessed Abraham richly for his wise choices. Abram thanked God for His blessings.

We also need to understand the consequences of Lot's poor choices and how he escaped with only the clothes he was wearing. Were the wages he received from his sin worth it? (Romans 6:23)

(First written by Iris and published in *Partners SS papers*, Christian Light Pub, 5.2002)

Where is Your Treasure Stored?

When we think of animals who store food, the bushy-tailed squirrel comes to mind. Squirrels don't store all their nuts together in a single location as some may think. They bury each nut a few inches under the ground in a separate hole. Squirrel watchers say when nuts are abundant the squirrel works every morning for several months until he buries about 10,000 nuts.

Amazingly, in winter months the squirrel finds the nuts easily. Even in deep snow a scent mechanism takes him directly to each spot. Nuts, not eaten that winter, sprout and grow, producing groves of nut trees. Nuts still buried that don't sprout, will decay or mold and have no value.

Squirrels are considered to be intelligent animals in caring for their own needs. God made them with great ability to adapt better than most animals. They change their diet in different seasons, from nuts to fruits, berries, wild honey, pine seeds, cones, tree buds, and bark. They cleverly steal food from squirrel-proof bird feeders.

God gave squirrels a bushy tail as protection from cold, rain, or icy weather. The tail also helps maintain balance when going from branch to branch. Squirrels dart around tree trunks to hide from potential enemies. A squirrel can imitate a cat to warn his friends of an approaching animal or other danger. His chirping warns that a cat is lurking nearby.

The Bible encourages people to save food for a rainy day or a nonproductive season, but God also told Christians to store up treasures in Heaven. Treasures stored on earth won't last through all eternity. They may outlast a person, but will be destroyed in the end. Earthly treasures can't be taken to heaven with the Christian. No one ever sees a

U-haul trailer being pulled behind a hearse. Over time, weather, moths, and rust will corrupt earthly treasures. All work done for earthly reasons will add up to zero. We need to think of God's eternal purpose for being on this earth.

Treasures stored in heaven will last forever. To store treasures in heaven you first need to know the Savior and do what He commands. We need to think about God's eternal purposes. These may include winning people to Christ, sharing, loving, encouraging, and helping others.

The Groundhog's Predictions

The brown **groundhogs** or woodchucks don't store food in their burrows or in the ground, but in their body fat. They dig burrows in the ground with their sharp front claws. The hind feet are used for scraping the dirt out of the hole. They keep clean rooms in their living quarters, one for sleeping and one for waste products. Many times they are seen sitting upright listening for danger, whistling, or looking for good food.

In most of northeastern United States and Canada groundhogs are destructive to buildings and their holes present a danger to large animals and people that break their legs falling in them. On farms and in neighborhoods groundhogs eat lots of gardens and crops, as well as fruit from orchards. Before going into hibernation for the winter groundhogs eat a lot, doubling their weight to a little more than ten pounds. In winter they live off the fat stored in their bodies and don't come out of the borrow until spring

About a month after the end of the winter sleep they have 4 or 5 young ones who are born blind, naked, and helpless. The parents care for them for at least a month until they can come out of the burrow and start eating plants.

February 2 is a day when people believe the groundhog comes out of hibernation to see his shadow. Some groups or clubs help the groundhogs come out of his burrow on February Second. Two groups noted in Pennsylvania newspapers sponsor Punxatawney Phil (Western PA) and Quarryville Orphie (Eastern PA). The Club says, *If the groundhog sees his shadow, he goes back to sleep and winter will last six more weeks. If he doesn't see his shadow, he starts his springtime activities and we can expect an early spring.*

This belief is a superstition. Christian people should avoid belief in superstitious ideas and good luck charms. They should put their trust in God for each day's activities and know He will care for His children. God put an amazing verse as the middle verse in the Bible. I don't believe He put it there by accident.

Look at Psalms 118:8, "It is better to trust in the LORD than to put confidence in man (people)." Fill in some of the same words in Jeremiah 17:7, "Blessed is the man (person) who _____ in the LORD, and whose hope (confidence) is in the _____."

A Smelly Defense
(*Based on true incidents*)

Striped Skunk

Most people recognize the little black skunk with white stripes and a long bushy tail, sometimes called a pole cat. However, in other places in the world skunks are about the size of a house cat and do not have the white stripe. It moves about slowly during the nights throughout North America.

One dark night I went out back of the barn to get my meowing kitten. I almost picked up the cat when I saw a light spot shining in the moonlight. When I felt the tail I realized it was the wrong kitty. I ran in the opposite direction and was fortunate not to get sprayed.

A frightened skunk can spray a vile-smelling scent up to ten feet with excellent aim. Their defense comes from a pair of scent glands near the tail. People stay away because of the unpleasant odor which clings. Many times the family dog had to be put out of the house because he tangled with a skunk. The family had to bathe him in gallons of tomato juice and vanilla to help eliminate the smell.

During the day the skunk sleeps in its den found in hollow trees, burrows, caves, or under old buildings. Skunks also sleep through most of the winter, but don't really hibernate like bears.

In spite of what people think, skunks aren't always the farmer's enemy. They kill and eat insects, rats, mice, and small animals which damage crops, but they do eat eggs and sometimes the farmer's chickens.

When I was young I raised the baby chickens on our small farm. Each of the mother hens *stole their nest* and sat on the eggs for twenty-one days until the little chicks hatched. Each hen had a different number of chicks and had to be put in a separate coop because each mother hen wouldn't accept the chicks another hen hatched. They usually picked them to death.

When the young chicks are about two months old the mother leaves them to return to the adult flock, lay more eggs, and eventually hatch out another brood if she can hide her nest where the egg gatherer cannot find them.

One night a skunk ripped the side off our cheaply made coop and pulled one of the young pullets (teenage hen) through the hole. The next night the skunk grabbed a young chicken by the wing ripping it out of the socket. In the morning I found her still safe in the coop with her siblings, even though she was minus a wing. I cared for her wound over the next weeks until she was healed.

This young pullet became a good egg layer, producing an egg every day for the rest of her life. However, she never stole her nest and tried to hatch out any baby chicks. Perhaps, God gave her the sensibility to realize she couldn't care for them with only one wing. Even the Bible tells the purpose of the hen's wings. (See Matthew 23:37b; Luke13:34.)

God wanted to protect Israel like a hen gathers her chicks under her wings, but they refused. In Psalms 91:4 we can trust in His promise to protect us under His wings like a hen protects her chicks. He wants us to trust in His promise.

The Donkey Made a Difference

Our hyperactive six-month old baby mule didn't permit any one to ride him. His speedy activities entertained us, as well as the horses, four times his size. They watched as he darted under the bottom fence rail and disappeared from their peering gaze. When he was two years old he calmed down enough to be a race horse's companion, but not dependable to carry a rider.

However, for thousands of years, donkeys have served humans in many parts of the world. A donkey crossed with a mare (female horse) produces a mule, a stronger work animal, used on many farms. A mule cannot reproduce another mule. Mules have a reputation of being stubborn and dull, but this is true only when they've been badly treated. Mules are very dependable workers. Mules will work very hard, but will stop when they have exerted all their strength. A horse will pull until he kills himself.

The donkey, a small, swift, sure-footed animal, was one of the first to be tamed. Larger breeds are used as pack animals, pulling heavy loads, while lighter breeds carry people. Females produce quality milk used by North Africans. A donkey requires less food than its larger, stronger relative—the horse. This makes the donkey cheaper to keep for work purposes.

People assume that a donkey carried the mother of Jesus to Bethlehem, although the Bible doesn't say for sure. Since Mary and Joseph had to walk about eighty miles from Nazareth to Bethlehem, Mary wouldn't have been able to walk the distance with the baby's birth so close. If

Joseph could have afforded it, he probably rented a donkey to carry her. At least a donkey is pictured in most Christmas scenes.

Later in Jesus' life he needed a donkey to ride into Jerusalem. He sent the disciples to get an unbroken colt of a donkey. This donkey was untrained, but with the Lord in control, it responded as if it had been broken. Sometimes we need to serve the Lord without much training, but our best preparation is daily prayer time spent with Him asking for His strength and wisdom.

Like the donkey, we should carry Him to Bethlehem or Jerusalem (our town and beyond), and make Him known to others we meet at school, work, or play. If submitted to His control, miracles can be performed through us.

Many times we feel weak, but God is strong…stronger than any earthly creature. We can trust Him to give us His strength to complete any task He has for us to do.

Donkeys were made to carry burdens, but many people carry heavy burdens unnecessarily. Just as our Lord and Master wants to take away our load of sin, He is able to carry every burden if we let Him. What a privilege to give our burdens to Him and trust Him to work out the answers!

Some donkeys and mules behave stubbornly because of man's mistreatment, but really we Christians have no excuse to be stubborn or disobedient because we have a kind Master—One who loved us so much that He died on the cross for our sins. Rightfully, we should desire to serve Him faithfully and obediently wherever we are—at school, at work, or at play.

Why are we stubborn and resist a magnificent God who loves us? It makes no sense why we close our ears so we can't hear God speak (Psalms 32:9)

(Written by Iris and Published in *Partners Sunday School Papers* –11.2001.)

HORSES

The Faithful Horse

The horse—a large, swift, and powerful animal—is man's useful friend. Horses do difficult jobs according to their size and breeding. They've served people for centuries. During training, horses learn obedience and submission with the use of a bit and bridle. Throughout history horses fought with their masters in battle, carried them over rough terrain, and pulled heavy loads. The bit and bridle teaches the horse to be obedient. The bit in the horse's mouth controls his will because of the mouth pain he feels.

(Psalm 32:8, 9; James 3:3. Look at a bit and bridle and discuss how they work.)

Today people ride horses for pleasure. Some horses still pull buggies to take their Amish masters to get food and supplies. Some are driven to church, to the doctor, or for an afternoon of pleasure. Other horses work daily in the fields. Whether past or present, most horses spend their lives faithfully serving people.

God created all animals and people to serve and bring Him pleasure. God gave different abilities, talents and jobs for animals to use in many different ways. He also gives different abilities, talents, and jobs to His people to use for His purposes. Unlike the forced submission of a horse, God permits people to submit their time, life, and talents voluntarily for His service.

In earlier times, the horse transported his master to church. Likewise, we should not forget to use our modern-day horse power to drive our own families and our unsaved friends to church, where we together can learn more about the Almighty God, who became a voluntary servant to all people.

(First written by Iris and published in *Partners Sunday school papers,* Christian Light Pub., 5.2002.)

Seeking Whom He May Devour

The lion, a symbol of power and beauty, is known as the "King of beasts." This large and powerful cat can weigh more than 400 pounds and can be nine feet long from their nose to the tip of their tail. They like to live in sparsely wooded areas with lots of animals, tall grass, and water nearby. Their tan coloring is protected by the yellowish brown color of dead grass.

Male lions are larger than the females and sleep 75% of the time. They like to sleep in the trees or tall grass where other animals can't see them. They grow a mane in the first five years of life which makes them look ferocious.

Females are slightly smaller than males and do most of the hunting. They have the first cubs about three to four years of age and every two years following. The spotted cubs drink milk for a few months and start eating meat after that. The mother stalks and kills the meat and teaches the cubs to hunt. All the lions in the pride feed on the prey she kills.

The lion has muscular shoulders and forelegs giving the great strength for clutching and holding the larger prey down. The pointed sharp teeth can quickly tear an animal's flesh apart.

The lion in mentioned many times in the Bible; for example, Jesus is called the Lion of the tribe of Judah. (a picture of his kingship). David believed that he was prepared by God to kill the giant, Goliath, when he killed the lion and bear that preyed on his sheep. (I Samuel 17:34, 35).

Wouldn't you be careful if you thought a lion were following you day and night? Really, one does follow us constantly. (I Peter 5:8) The devil with his lion nature is going about seeking whom he may devour. He is watching for each chance to keep us from living for the Lord. He loves to accuse us before God of wrong we have done. We should be thankful that Jesus died to cleanse us from our sins and is at God's right hand to ask forgiveness for us. Remember, the devil is the evil one. (Take _d_ off of _devil,_ and you spell _evil_.) The devil really is the evil one.

Daniel, chapter 6 tells one of the greatest Bible stories involving lions. Daniel had spent his life serving God and praying to Him, even though he lived in a foreign pagan land where few people worshiped God in heaven. Because Daniel continued to worship God, He made Daniel a success and gave him in a place of leadership in this foreign kingdom. Daniel's accusers were jealous of Daniel. They tricked the king into making a law that all people had to bow down to him three times a day or be cast into the lion's den. Being a proud king, he made this irrevocable law.

Of course, Daniel continued to pray to God three times a day where they could see him, as he always did. The accusers watched for their chance and reported him to the king. The King was very upset because he had high respect for Daniel, but he had to carry out his law. He hoped Daniel's God would deliver his faithful servant.

King Darius spent a miserable night worrying while Daniel kept company with lions whose mouths were shut by his God in Heaven (Daniel 6:16)

In the morning the king anxiously went to the lion's den and found Daniel without a scratch. He acknowledged that Daniel's God was the real true and living God. The king commanded that all the accusers and their families be thrown into the lion's den. You should read what the hungry lion's did to them. (Daniel 6: 16-28)

Why are we afraid to pray in public or are afraid of what the devil and his friends can do to us. God has shown in Daniel's life what He can do for us if we trust Him.

In Daniel, chapter 6, how many times did Daniel pray in spite of the kings ruling against it? _____. Do you think the lions were hungry when they saw Daniel? _____ Prove it.

A Life in Darkness
(the mole)

Common Mole

"Why is this ground so humpy and bumpy?" Katie asked as she kept sinking into the soft mounds of earth.

"That's the damage a mole has done to my yard," said Grandpa.

"What is a mole and why do they make these humps?" asked Katie.

"A mole is a small mammal that burrows underground. Its head is wedge-shaped and its ears aren't visible, but they hear well. Its tiny nearly blind eyes are covered by skin because it doesn't need to see where it lives. Its large forelegs and long broad paws dig burrows. These paws work like shovels scooping out the earth, helping the mole do quite a good job of spoiling my lawn and garden," said Grandpa.

"Does it have baby moles underground?" asked Katie.

"It has a family nest several feet down, but it searches for worms and insects in the tunnels closer to the surface of the earth. One good thing, it only eats a small amount of plantlife. Adult moles can be as small as six inches or as large as fourteen inches."

"Wow! That's pretty big! No wonder this yard is so bumpy," said Katie rather astonished.

"The mole doesn't need good eyes. It's happy to live in its dark underground home. Too many people seem like the mole. They seem happy living in darkness. They don't realize they are living in spiritual darkness away from God. Some people live in darkness all their lives because they have never had the light of the Word of God to expose their sin.

"Once people understand what sin is and that they were born in sin, they begin to see a need to get out of darkness into light. Until a person realizes they need to ask forgiveness for their sins, their eyes are like the moles, covered with overhanging skin, keeping them from seeing the light of Jesus.

"People who know Jesus, no longer enjoy the old life and its darkness. Our lives change from that old life to one of righteousness and light. God wants us to be a beacon of light to those who are blind," related Grandpa.

"That's interesting. Now I know why I can see so many sinful, evil things people do," said Katie.

"Yes, people don't realize what's right or wrong until God opens their blind eyes and reveals it to them. We need to pray God will help people see with spiritual eyes and not eyes covered with darkness and blindness," explained Grandpa.

Paul (Saul) thought he was doing what was right by killing Christians, but on the road to Damascus God blinded him with a great light. He was physically blind, but became spiritually able to see. He heard _ _ _ _ _ call to him. He saw the *Light of the World*. After this experience Paul's life changed to one of serving God. Acts 9:5

When we go to a country that doesn't speak our language, we feel lost and wonder around like a blind person. In some countries people read from the bottom of the page and from right to left. Try that method with these letters and see what you did not see.

e e s I w o n t u b, d n i l b s a w, d n u o f m a w o n t u b, t s o l s a w e c n o l; e m e k i l h c t e r w a d e v a s t a h t, d n u o s e h t t e e w s w o h, e c a r g g n i z a m a <--- *(start here and write the letters below)*

_____

_____

_____

_____

Earthworms Need Air

"Mom, did you see those earthworms all over the sidewalk and in the puddles? Why are there so many on a rainy morning?" asked Ethan.

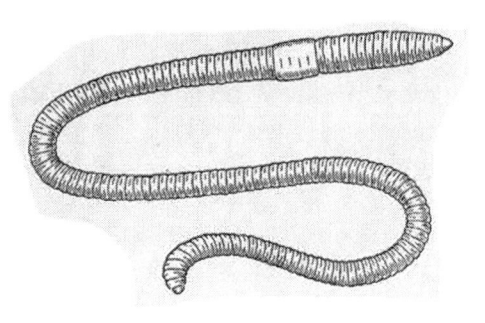

"Earthworms usually burrow in the soil. They feed on dead plant material. They chew, digest, and excrete plant matter that nourishes the soil."

"Let me explain how earthworms help the farmers and gardeners. Plants need air around their roots; this is important for the plant's growth. Air enters soil through the burrows dug by earthworms that need air to stay alive. In hot, dry conditions earthworms need to breathe through a thin skin layer which is helped by contact with the air spaces in the soil. During heavy rain those air spaces fill with water," answered Mother.

"Oh! They come up where we can see them to keep from drowning," said Ethan.

"That's right. When the ground is saturated all the air disappears. Haven't you seen bubbles come up to the top of the water when you throw a chuck of sod in the pond?" added Mother.

"Unlike the earthworms which die saturated in water, Christians can become more alive and spiritual if saturated in God's Word. There is no danger of drowning by reading and meditating on God's Word, unless the reader does not apply God's principles in his life. The Bible is God's inspired Word, not just a history or literature book as taught by some teachers. God promised His Word will not return unto Him void.

Bookworms, who have an undying thirst for reading, resemble earthworms which constantly digest plant matter in the soil. Just as earthworms can't survive without air and food, the bookworm can't survive without books and reading. Christians need to be like earthworms—living, eating, and digesting God's Word. Digesting means more than reading. It includes studying, meditating, and applying Bible principles to our lives. When we make the Word a part of our life we can nurture others who need help understanding the Bible. We need to study it, meditate on it, apply it in our lives, and give out its nourishment to others who need help.

"Earthworms provide food for some birds and also make good bait for a fisherman who needs to catch his dinner. Some fishermen like larger earthworms called *night crawlers*. With a flashlight we found night crawlers on the lawn at night. We gathered them and sold them to fishermen.

"Once we children made a fishing pole out of an old stick and a hook out of a safety pin attached to a piece of string. With this makeshift pole and a night crawler we caught a fourteen inch bass. From this experience we learned how God made some animals a unique part of the food chain."

Who Do We Imitate?

"Polly wants a cracker." We've all heard those words said by a parrot or crow. Some birds have been taught to imitate people. These birds have more ability to imitate and remember sounds than others.

The slate gray catbird, a mockingbird relative, sings delightful music by imitation. The catbird, a dull colored bird, about nine or ten inches long, often makes a mewing sound. Fooled listeners look for a lost cat. The mewing, which earned the name catbird, gets louder when the bird is scared.

The catbird gets a poor reputation because it likes to eat the farmer's berry crops, making up for less than half of its diet. A better reputation is earned by eating harmful beetles, ants, crickets, and caterpillars. The parent birds feed their young a diet of over ninety percent insects. One of the catbird's greatest contributions is destruction of the gypsy moth pest.

It seems that whatever the catbird does is to the best of its ability whether imitating beautiful songs, feeding its young, or helping the farmer. We, as Christians, should please God by giving our best in all we do, see, and say. We should also watch who and what we imitate. In these days of television, i-phones, and computer internet there is so much that enters our minds through the eye-gate. Being careful in these matters brings glory to God, as well as, being an example for others to follow.

Christian parents should imitate the catbird's lesson by feeding their children the best physical food, along with daily spiritual food.

When God created the catbird he gave it the unique ability to repeat musical imitations, which please listeners. We, as Christians, can please God by singing God-honoring music and imitating a Christ-like life and attitude.

Our life and language should reflect Jesus' compassionate love, humility, forgiveness, gentleness, kindness, and patience. God is pleased when we keep our eyes on our Savior. It is obvious to those around us whether our actions imitate His. (Galatians 5:22, 23)

(First published in *Partners SS papers*)

Important to God

"You are worth more than many Sparrows." (Matthew 10:31)

Sparrows are one of the most common birds in the world. There are more than 500 species. Sparrows are small, averaging five to eight inches in length. The song sparrow has more than 72 species in North America.

Most sparrows have dull body colors, with brighter-colored markings on the head. The dull color of the sparrows protects them in the marshy or brushy surroundings where they live. Sparrows are usually found very close to the ground or in high grasses where they make their cup-shaped nests. When danger approaches they fake injury to lead the enemy away from the nest. Some species pump their tails vigorously and sing a scolding song to defend their home.

The food of the sparrow is mostly injurious insects and weed seeds. In this sense they're helpful to farmers and gardeners. Sparrows usually like to stay away from places that are heavily inhabited by humans. There are so many species of sparrows, and they're not as colorful as other birds, so humans sometimes think of them as annoying.

Has anyone ever told you that you were annoying? Well, you know what? Just let them know that God doesn't think you are annoying. God created the many species of sparrows and cares what happens to each one of them. That means that He cares even more for you.

Think about it. God cares for the sparrows' needs. He gave them inconspicuously colored feathers for warmth and protection, and created a short beak for crunching seeds and harmful insects. Now, why would God do all of that if He thought they were annoying?

The Bible talks about taking care of our needs. In Isaiah 58:11 it says, "The Lord will guide you always; he will satisfy your needs." Now, that doesn't mean He'll give you everything you ask for, but He will take care of what is important.

The next time you wonder if God is really out there, let the sparrow remind you that not only is He out there, but He is taking care of your needs as well.

(First published in *Kid's Ministry Ideas*, Jan.-March, 2003).

Does A Praying Mantis Really Pray or Prey?

The praying mantis, a gardener's friend, helps rid our gardens, flower beds, and fields of destructive insects. Most adult praying mantises are about three to four inches long and have protective coloring of green and brown. The name came from its resemblance to someone in a praying position. Being the only insect able to turn its head over its shoulder to spot and capture another insect makes the praying mantis unique. This insect shows one more example of God's creative genius and Master plan.

The adults can be seen among the plants until cold weather appears. The female lays a tan, foamy-looking egg mass on the thick stems of plants. With the job of reproducing completed, the adults die. A wise gardener must be alert to look carefully for the egg masses when cleaning the flower beds and gardens, taking care not to throw away next year's helpers. Bringing them into a warm room will cause them to emerge too early, so putting them in the refrigerator until late spring will retard the hatching. The wise gardener should attach the stem containing the nest to a strong stake and place them in the flower beds around his house so the mantises can hatch naturally. Be careful to keep them away from any known ant mounds because ants love to make a tasty dessert of mantis eggs.

When the spring weather turns warmer about a hundred little mantises hatch from the egg mass. The babies, about a half inch long, start to search for food immediately before some hungry bird gobbles them up. It's difficult for a young mantis to survive, but with a daily diet of insects they will grow rapidly. They really do prey on other insects.

What a practical example of how important a daily spiritual diet of God's Word and prayer are to the Christian. We can grow rapidly or very slowly depending on how much spiritual nourishment we receive. Without God's daily diet we won't grow and serve God effectively. Think of fifteen-year-old Daniel and his friends who chose God's diet over the pagan Kings expensive food. They grew to be healthier than those that ate the King's food (Daniel 1).

Interestingly, "*Newsweek* reported a Chicago High School removed a praying mantis from its biology collection as a result of the 1963 Supreme Court decision against prayer and Bible reading in the public schools. The devil and his followers definitely know prayer is the Christian's source of power. How much more should we, who know the Lord, recognize the power of prayer. Missionaries say their work would be severely hampered if we only gave material support and forgot to pray." God wants us to always be ready to use His great sources of strength and power, much like Daniel did in the pagan land of Babylon.

When I was a student and young teacher every school day started with Bible Reading and Prayer. In 1963 Madalyn Murray O'Hair, founder of *American Atheists*, influenced the U.S. Supreme Court ruling to end official Bible-reading, prayer, and discussion of God in American public schools (*Murray v. Curlett lawsuit*). A window of freedom was lost at that moment.

What has changed in 50 years? God and His Word did not change. God's Word still is and always has been inspired, infallible, and truthful. However, it isn't difficult to note that our children, families, and educational system have changed. Some people no longer want God's Word or its influence. Respect for authority has diminished. To the wise historian it is clear that wrong decisions have consequences. We have been observing these results in our schools, homes, and communities up to and after the turn of the century.

Bibliography: *Insects, Golden Nature Guide.* Murray, William J. *My Life without God*, p. 91.

Can you Smell that Stink Bug?

The brown stink bug was accidently introduced into the United States from either China or Japan. The bugs probably hid as stowaways in packing crates and were discovered near Allentown, Pennsylvania in September 1998. They quickly spread over Southeastern Pennsylvania then to neighboring states. The bug was found in New Jersey in 2000, and other surrounding states in the next few years, in states south of the Mason-Dixon line in 2009, and in the mid-western states and Oregon in 2010. By 2011 it spread to as many as 34 states in the United States.

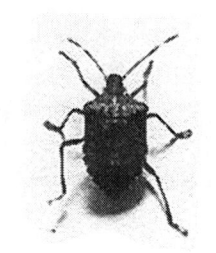

This stinky insect is about three-fourths of an inch long, shaped like a shield, and resembles a squash bug. It has stink glands on the underside of the thorax used as a defense mechanism to keep birds and lizards from having it for dinner. This bug has become an uncontrollable agricultural pest.

The stink bug causes widespread damage to the fruit and vegetable crops, such as peaches, apples, pears, green beans, soybeans, cherry, raspberries, tomatoes, corn, etc. The Pennsylvania apple and peach crops have been especially hard hit. This annoying pest pierces its proboscis into the fruit, sucks out the juice, and deposits saliva that causes rotting and corking of the flesh underneath. Spoilage occurs more rapidly than usual. (I personally noticed the difference in my apple crop in 2010 to 2012. I had apples in storage until April from the harvest of 2011, but in 2012 my apples didn't last until Christmas. I noticed the brown marks on both apples and pears, but didn't realize the reason until writing this article.)

"How did this insect spread so rapidly, you ask?" In the fall the stink bug squeezes into houses around the window and door frames, into soffits, under the siding, through broken screens, through ceiling fans, through cracks in baseboards, or wherever they can find a crevice to sneak in. It hibernates as an adult in our homes over the winter. Stink bugs don't usually hurt humans, just annoy them as they liven up in the warmth of your home. However, a few bites have been reported and allergies and rashes have been caused by the secretion from their bodies. They can produce two to six families a year. The number an adult produces increases with warmer weather conditions.

I have discovered that praying mantises eat the stink bug, but while the mantis is devouring the first bug, I watched the others quickly disappear. The praying mantises near my house became very fat with brownish stomachs from eating so many. When they became stuffed and left the screen door, the stink bugs came back. Each Fall I am going to continue saving the praying mantis egg cases to produce more mantises to help me with my garden and fruit trees each spring and summer.

Research is in progress to control these pests. Sprays are not much help in controlling them. They outlast the potency of the spray and too much spray can cause damage to humans whether it's used indoors or outside in the yards and fields. Be careful or the sprays may kill helpful insects. At present there are a few helpful predators which kill stink bugs: one species of spider, praying mantises, and a wasp.

I heard of another method in the home. Stink bugs do not like water and will drown, so here are some inexpensive ways to eliminate them. Fill a spray bottle with water, window cleaner, and dish detergent. If you can find areas they sneak in, spray those areas with this moisture. Gather the bugs that try to share your residence and put them in a plastic container. Saturate them with this dish water spray. They seem to drown after a few minutes. If you notice a lot of bugs in one area, put this mixture in a wide-mouthed container and hold it below the bugs. Watch as the bugs fall into the mixture. To save water, wait until you have a number in the container, then flush them down the toilet.

I noted the bug has a crusty thorax shaped like a shield. In the Middle Ages shields were used to protect the body of a soldier as he fought with a sword or spear. The shield protected his vital organs against the charging enemy. In the Bible when David went to fight against the nine-foot giant, King Saul gave him his own armor for protection. The armor weighed the young David down so much that he couldn't carry it into the battle, so he laid it aside to use his faith and trust in God. God directed him to use a small sling-shot and three small stones. God guided the stone to the right spot to kill that defiant giant—proof that God's shield of faith works. David wrote in Psalms 28:7 *"The Lord is my strength and my shield…"*

In many other Old Testament battles God told the Israelites that he was their shield and buckler. He would go before them and protect them in the battle if they would be obedient and trust Him. In Psalms 91:4 God reminds them: *"His truth shall be thy shield and buckler."*

A shield is also a symbol of protection to the Christian believer. Paul wrote to the Christians at Ephesus about needing the whole armor of God to fight against the ways of the devil (Ephesians 6:10-17). Paul mentioned the *breastplate of righteous* and the *shield of faith* for protection against the fiery darts or tricks of the devil.

Just as the stink bug finds ingenious ways to get into our homes and buildings, we Christians need to be aware of the devils subtle ways in getting into our lives and bringing about little sins which will grow and eventually take over. These subtle entries of nasty words, bullying, gossip, dirty jokes, porno pictures, lying, deceiving, stealing, revenge, and hatred can increase with time. We need to watch the subtle influences that come by the newest cell phones, computers, TV, and movies. We do need to use God's shield of faith to avoid these captivating invasions.

Just as the stink bug gives off a pungent odor, God doesn't want the Christian to give off an odor which would make people walk away from Him. It is God's desire that a Christian gives off a sweet-smelling savor that will make people want to follow Him and be secure in His protection. It seems the stink bug has a life of destruction which is not what God wants for us. He wants us to bring glory to Himself with a life of kindness, love, peacemaking, encouragement, listening, praying, and helping others.

(Reference) http://Wikipedia.brown stink bug.com
http://www.ehow.com/info_stink-bugs-house

An Insect that is Not Lazy!

There are many kinds of ants living in all parts of the world except near the poles. Ants are small pests, but numerous invaders of homes, yards, and gardens. Ants do not live alone, but most live and work together in colonies to provide food for the entire colony. They can be found under rocks and in borrows in the ground. There are usually hundreds in a colony.

The colonies are somewhat like cities. Some feed and care for the young. Others keep the nest clean or store away food and others guard the entrances to the nest. They may invade other nests especially of the honey bee, honey dew aphids, and praying mantis egg case, as well as other ant's nests, because they like to eat and store sweet foodstuffs. An ant can carry loads many times heavier than itself. Ants do bite.

There are many species of ants that differ in many ways from other species. Some like carpenter ants can be destructive to wood buildings and trees. Some like the fire ants can cause serious injury or even death to a person or animal.

One of the smallest ants is called the Pharaoh ant. They make a path into homes or wherever they can find food. It seems that ants are ambitious, wise, and hard workers. It is said they store food in the summer and fall for winter. They spend the winter sleeping inside their nests.

Ants are mentioned several places in the Bible as being industrious insects. God gives the contrast of other animals that do not prepare ahead and so die without food. The Bible calls ants wise because of preparations they make. It also warns people to be like the ant and not the sluggard because laziness will bring a person to poverty and a sad end (Proverbs 6:6-11).

There is a fable about the lazy grasshopper as compared to the industrious ant. Laziness is not a characteristic God likes. He warns us about laziness and its consequences.

To cross a stream, some ants form a living bridge from a twig, blade of grass, or large hanging leaf. Other ants walk over the bridge in search of food or a new home. This reminds me of the bridge Jesus Christ made for us to reach the home he prepared for us in heaven. Because of our sins we cannot get to heaven in our own goodness. Sin made a chasm between us and God. That's why we need the perfect man Jesus who took our sins on Himself at the cross of Calvary. We can be forgiven just by asking for His forgiveness. Jesus is the bridge God provided so we can cross into Heaven when we die and be with Him forever.

Bee A Faithful Worker

Honeybee colonies show an example of insects working together to preserve a family. Three types of bees make up the family. One queen and the male drones help produce new workers. These workers do all the chores to keep the hive operating.

Beware of the guards! A few worker bees guard the hive's entrance against enemies. Each hive has its own odor sensed by the guard bees. They know a stranger bee, animal, or man.

Bees can return to their own hive without restraint. A strange bee will be stopped. These faithful workers have one stinger and die if they need to use it.

Honeybee guards are alert when intruders get too close. They're ready at a moment's notice to give their life to protect the growing family. They will not let a stranger leave without feeling their presence. (Ref: World Book Encyclopedia.)

King Josiah sent his trusted helper to the temple to get the money that the doorkeepers collected from the people. He ordered the money to be used to pay the carpenters, masons, and builders to repair the temple of the Lord. He trusted them to work together faithfully just like the faithful workers in a beehive.

The high priest found the Book of the Law and gave it to the secretary, who quickly read it to the king. King Josiah, a very young king, asked the religious leaders to find out what it meant. As a faithful leader he responded with humility and renewed the covenant with the Lord.

Sometimes God uses young people to perform a difficult task. For generations the Israelites had worshipped idols. Now this youthful king ordered all idols, and shrines to be torn down and burned. He vowed to do right in God's sight even if it cost him his kingdom or his life. God was pleased when King Josiah and his people pledged to follow Him with all their heart and soul. (Read 2 Chronicles 34)

Thankful for Fleas?

Corrie ten Boom told about the torturous fleas in the infested Nazi concentration camps of WW2. She and her sister, along with other innocent prisoners, endured the pesky fleas. Later, they discovered the fleas were a blessing in disguise. The guards let them pray, sing hymns, and study the Bible because they didn't want to step inside the barracks for fear of getting nasty flea bites. Corrie and her sister thanked God for the fleas that brought freedom so they could worship. Would we think to thank God for something like a nasty flea?

Did you know the bubonic plague of the Middle Ages that killed millions of people was traced to fleas and rats? A number of other plagues in Europe and America have had similar causes. Some people believe that fleas also transmit Lyme disease.

Fleas, small wingless insects about one-eighth of an inch long, live on mammals and birds. They get their food from sucking the blood of the host and are dangerous because they spread disease germs from infected animals, like rats and squirrels.

Fleas are pests to both humans and domesticated animals. They are strong, have great endurance, and can leap more than a foot. Fleas drop eggs all around the living quarters. Eggs hatch in a few weeks with no help from the parent. The babies find a host from which to get their food. It's an amazing fact that they can live up to 4 months without food and up to 18 months with occasional feeding and they don't stay on dead animals.

A flea, hard to find or get rid of, stays where there is life-giving blood. We, as Christians, need this kind of endurance. Sticking close and following Christ, who has the life-giving blood, will help us to grow spiritually. We need to stay close to Him even if we live in a palace or in a prison, like Corrie.

Fleas were common in Middle Eastern countries. I Samuel 26:20 mentioned that King Saul hunted David in the mountains like one hunts a flea on a partridge. That's how we should search for commands and promises in God's Word. Wherever we go or whatever we do we need to get our life, endurance, and victory from staying close to our Lord.

(Written by Iris and First published by *The Standard,* Word Action Publishers—9. 2005.)

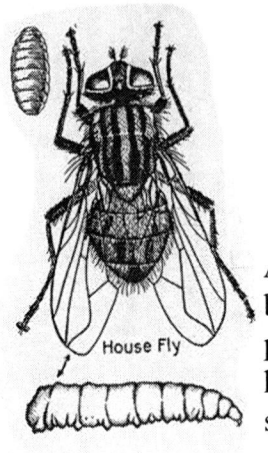

Getting Your Attention

As Amy sat in Sunday school class, a fly kept buzzing around her face, buzz-buzz-buzz. The pesky insect flitted around her head and buzzed in her ear. She batted at it wildly, but it flew to bother someone else for a minute, then back again.

The fly got all the attention. What the teacher said wasn't heard until she mentioned the thousands of pests God sent as plagues on Pharaoh and the Egyptians.

"Not one, but many thousands flew around their heads, buzzed in their ears, and sat on their food. Their houses and beds were filled with swarms of insects. Can you imagine how annoying that must have been?" said Mrs. Gold, the teacher.

"The millions of insects (flies, lice, locusts), God sent on the Egyptians, were only three ways God tried to get their attention. He wanted them to know He was the true and living God who had greater power than all the rulers and magicians of Egypt."

"I can't believe Pharaoh was so stubborn," Amy said. "He had to know the God of the Israelites was real and powerful. He had to know God meant what He said. But still he refused to do what God wanted and let the Israelites go."

"Finally, God got Pharaoh's attention by taking his first born son," the teacher said. "After that he let the Israelites go. There's no place recorded in the Bible where it says Pharaoh trusted in the God of Heaven."

It only took one fly to get your attention. For some, like Pharaoh, it takes more insects, or more disasters. How much will it take for us to trust and obey the living and true God of Heaven?"

Amy thought, *I'm not sure if God tried to get my attention or Satan tried to keep me from paying attention. In any case, it took only one fly for me to learn the power of the true God, who can use His creatures to get people's attention. He wants everyone to have a chance to know Him and trust His power. I'm not going to be stubborn like Pharaoh.*[1]

In Exodus 8 to 10 God tried to get Pharaoh's attention with ten plagues, so that he would let the Israelites go. Three plagues were insect pests: flies, lice, and locusts. Each species is described below: (Psalms105: 26-38)

There are many kinds of flies. One is the common house fly—an insect with two wings. It is a dangerous pest because it carries germs inside its body or on the body hair. With its bite, germs are also left. Some flies carry malaria, sleeping sickness, and typhoid fever. They not only cause disease in humans, but in animals and plants. A female fly produces thousands of eggs in her lifetime. Eggs hatch into rice-shaped larvae that eat, grow, and change into the pupa and adult stages. The larvae are called *maggots*. God created the *Flycatcher*, a species of bird, which helps control the pests of flies.

A louse is a small insect that sucks the sap of plants or blood of animals. Lice are parasites that attack other animals and plants. Plant lice are called aphids. God created many species of lady bugs who love to feast on aphids.

There are three kinds of lice that suck the blood of humans. A louse has hooked feet for hooking to hair. The eggs attached to hair are called *nits*. Lice are hard to get rid of, but once a person has head lice a strong solution is used to kill adults and eggs. Boiling water helps kill the lice and nits on beds, pillows, and clothes. Cleanliness is an important way to control these pests. Lice also spread typhus fever. All over the land of Egypt the "*dust* became lice." (Exodus 8:16-18).

---

[1] (The first 8 paragraphs of this story were written by Iris and published in *Shining Star Magazine*, Spring, 1998.)

Locusts, which look similar to grass hoppers, are brownish in color and about two inches long. They travel in swarms or large groups and destroy whole fields of crops at a time, by eating it. What the locusts do not eat they infect with a moisture from their body that kills the rest of the plant. One way scientists and farmers have learned to control the locusts pests, is by plowing in the fall. Turning over the soil destroys eggs which are laid in the soil. Birds also devour them.

The Bible mentions locusts in several places. In Exodus 10:14 locusts destroyed the crops of the Egyptians when Pharaoh would not let God's people go. In 2 Chronicles 7:13 God sent locusts to get the Israelites attention when they had turned away from Him. God permitted the locusts to be eaten by the Israelites (Leviticus 11:21, 22). What did John the Baptist eat in Mark 1:6? _____ and wild honey. In Revelation 9:3 teachers of false doctrine are likened to locusts that infect others with a poison.

A Special Touch
(How to Make a Moth or Butterfly Collection)

Near a busy store many people stopped and stared. I couldn't help but wonder what had gotten their attention. Much to my surprise, they spied a large rare spotted, orange moth with a wing span of four inches. The bricks provided protective coloration during the daylight when moths usually hide.

Royal Walnut Moth

Since this was the first Royal Walnut Moth I had ever seen, I felt an urge to save it for my collection. This would be a good one to study and show to my Science classes. I read in the Insect Guide that moths don't live long after mating and depositing their eggs. This prompted me to capture my prey in a spare bag. Immediately, it fluttered trying to escape.

When I arrived home I put the moth in a small container in the freezer. This would quiet its activity and keep the wings pliable when thawed. Pliable wings are easily mounted.

Since a moth rests with its wings horizontal, the fore wings have to be stretched upward by attaching strips of card paper over them until they become dry and permanent. (See figure 3 on page 75) Be careful using tape as it may cause loss of color and destroy parts of the wings. Craft pins make handling easier. This stage requires a special skillful touch only acquired by practice. Next, store the body in an airtight box with moth balls to prevent hatching of eggs previously laid on its body by another moth or insect.

After a few weeks remove the paper strips. The wings will be crisp and dry, so handle carefully with the pins. Next prepare a permanent mounting case. If you don't have money to buy one, an inexpensive flat box covered with clear plastic can be used. Place moth crystals under a thin layer of Styrofoam or layer of cotton polyester. With pins, attach the moth to the styrofoam. As an important finishing touch, label each specimen, cover with clear plastic, and seal tightly. The lid serves as protection for storage.

While studying these beautiful insects we can learn about God as the creator. Raising a moth through its metamorphosis shows how unique each is. The mother lays eggs on the dinner table of the Creator's choice. Each baby caterpillar eats a different plant and can only survive on a specific food supply. For example, the Imperial caterpillars feed on hickory, oak, and maple leaves; the Royal Walnut caterpillars eat hickory, sumac, and sweet gum leaves; the Cecropia larvae feeds on cherry or maple, and so on. None will crossbreed or go against God's design for it. Refer to the *Butterfly/Moth Insect Guide*.[1]

Mounting is fun, but should be done with a purpose. Keep a notebook of your findings using a variety of projects. As you observe, study, and record, you will add a profitable finishing touch to your collection. Wouldn't you like to have that special finishing touch? Draw and color a moth like the one in the story.

---

[1] Mitchell, R. & Zim, H. *Golden Guide of Butterflies & Moths*, Golden Press, NY.

In the 1940s and early 1950s there were no plastic bags and children didn't have much money to buy fancy mounting cases. I used cardboard boxes about 12x12x1 inches deep with a lid. I sprinkled moth crystals under a layer of cotton batting my mother used to make quilts. After pinning the specimen to the cotton with its labeling information I used a hot iron to seal cellophane around the box so it would be air tight. This would keep other insects from laying eggs on the bodies in my collection box, much like a moth lays eggs in our wool clothes. Some eggs were laid on the bodies before you put them in the box, so the moth crystals will kill those pests. I got the idea of using the hot iron and cellophane because I had watched my parents seal the meat for the freezer in that way.

These insect collections described above still exist in these boxes in the year 2012. They are over 60 years old. The cellophane dried up and split so I replaced it with plastic bags when they were widely used in the 1960s. I also started preserving the specimens in a freezer container in the first stage. The butterflies and moths do less destruction to their own wings when putting them in a Ziploc bag in the freezer .[2]

---

[2](The first 7 paragraphs by Iris were published in *Nature Friend Magazine-8.1996* & *God's World News—5.1998*)

What's on the Moth caterpillar's dinner table?

The different leaves each Moth caterpillar eats can be found in an Insect Guide. In the 1940s and early 1950s there were no plastic bags and children didn't have much money to buy fancy mounting cases. I used cardboard boxes about 12" by 12" by 1 inch deep, with a lid. I sprinkled moth crystals under a layer of cotton batting my mother used to make quilts. After pinning the specimen to the cotton with its labeling information I used a hot iron to seal cellophane around the box so it would be air tight. This would keep other insects from laying eggs on the bodies in my collection box, much like a moth lays eggs in our wool clothes. Some eggs were laid on the bodies before you put them in the box, so the moth crystals will kill those pests. I got the idea of using the hot iron and cellophane because I had watched my parents seal the meat for the freezer in this way.

[3] The insect collections described above still exist in the year 2012. They have been in the same boxes over 60 years. The cellophane dried up and split so I replaced it with plastic bags when they were invented in the 1960s. The butterflies and moths do less destruction to their own wings by putting them in Ziploc bags in the freezer to preserve a specimen in the first stage.

---

[3] The author is still available to show these 60 year-old collections and talk about insect collecting.

Additional Information about Moths and Butterflies:

1. What is on the Moth or Butterfly caterpillar's dinner table?
   - The different leaves each caterpillar eats can be found in the *Wildlife Insect Guides.* [4]

2. Divisions of the Caterpillar and Moth or Butterfly's body:
   - Head — has pair of antennae, eyes, sensory structures, mouth, coiled proboscis.
   - Thorax — three pairs of legs; breathing openings; two pairs of scaled, veined wings.
   - Abdomen — sex organs.

3. Stages of the metamorphosis cycle:
   - Egg — placed on leaves to hatch and eat.
   - Larva — caterpillar eats leaves, grows and molts its skin several times.

     — moth caterpillar spins a cocoon around itself using external materials.

     — A butterfly caterpillar spins a chrysalis around itself.
   - Pupa — transformed from caterpillar to adult: loses prolegs; wings develop;

     — chewing mandibles change to proboscis; reproductive organs form.
   - Adult — emerges from the cocoon/chrysalis with wings that expand as fluids are pumped through the veins; sucks nectar; carries pollen to other plants;

     — lays eggs on the leaves of choice.

4. Enemies of all stages of Moths and Butterflies Life:
   - Bacteria, fungi, protozoa, viruses attack caterpillars
   - Parasitic insects (some flies and wasp larva eat caterpillars)
   - Spiders catch and eat caterpillars and adults
   - Skunks, foxes, raccoons, opossums, mice, moles, shrews, squirrels, toads, frogs, lizards, and snakes eat them.
   - Man and unfavorable weather

5. Defenses against these many enemies:
   - Lays hundreds of eggs
   - Camouflage with surroundings
   - Body markings to frighten enemies
   - Hairs, spines, and tastes unpleasant to enemies

6. Hobbies to help study Moths and Butterflies:
   - Photograph specimens with zoom camera or video
   - Raise and observe living specimens
   - Collect, mount, and label specimens
   - Collect pictures from magazines and make a scrapbook
   - Label pictures and photos
   - Grow plants that attract larva and adults
   - Keep detailed records of observations
   - Answer questions: *what, where, when, why, how, how many*, and *how long*.

7. When on hunting expeditions, carry a dark plastic relaxing jar to lessen wing damage.

8. If the insect can't be mounted in a few hours, put it in the freezer to keep the wings pliable and easy to work with.

DIAGRAMS:

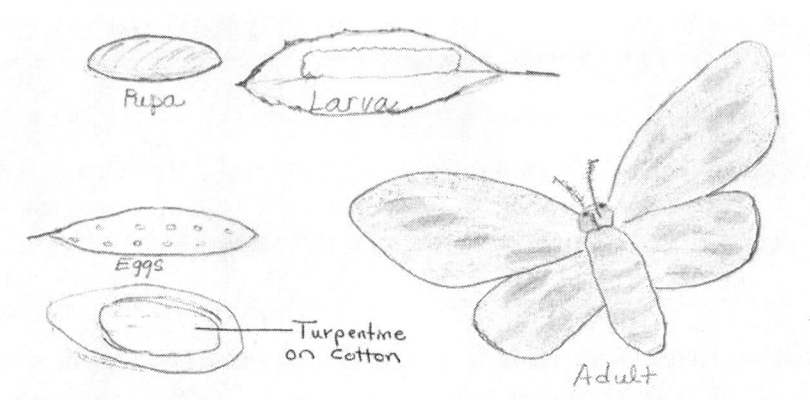

Figure 1--sleeping jar

Figure 2--Royal Walnut Moth

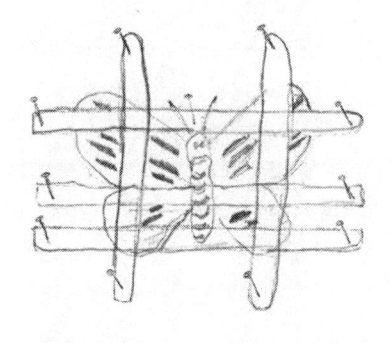

Figure 3--Setting and Mounting

Figure 4--Mounting Box

---

[4] Walker, Herbert. 1967. *A Moth Is Born,* Rand McNally Co., Chicago.

Cox, Rosamind K. *Usborne's First Nature Book, Butterflies and Moths,* EDC Pub, Tulsa, OK.

Stokes, Donald. 1991. *A Guide to Observing Insect Lives.* Boston, MA Little Brown.

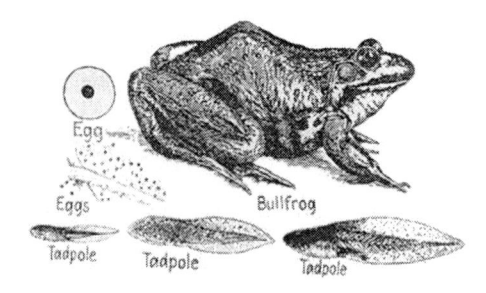

How the Tadpole Changes

A tadpole hatches from an egg laid in the water by the mother frog. In the next few weeks the tadpole goes through changes on the outside and inside while growing. Outside, it grows back legs and then front legs. Inside, the gills become lungs to help it breathe out of water. Finally the tadpole's tail shrinks as it develops into a "full-grown" **frog.** Now it can jump on land and swim in the water as it wishes, but it can't stay underwater without coming up for air.

Those of us who choose Jesus as our Savior also go through a change on the inside, as well as the outside. Jesus changes us from a sinner, bound for an eternity without Him, to a saint bound for heaven with Him. Our desires change to ones that will please the Lord. Sometimes these changes are immediate, but other times the change takes weeks, or months, or years as we continue to grow in Christ.

A changed person doesn't talk or act as he once did. His desire is to please God. Like the frog which swims in the water, a person still has the old nature and lives in the earthly world. But he is now a stranger in that world because his lifestyle has changed. God helps us make other needful changes even in the things we wear and also our facial expression. The frog has no choice in the matter of change, but God is honored and well pleased when we willingly choose to make changes in obedience to Him. We should desire to become more like his Son, Jesus, every day. [1]

---

[1] (The first 3 paragraphs of the Frog story were written by Iris and published in *Partners SS Papers*. Sept.2000. Reprinted in *Spiritual Voice*, 2003.)

In the Bible we read about two men whose lives were alike, in that, they were tax collectors, became wealthy publicans, were sinners, and had ability in figuring. Publicans were Jews who collected taxes for the Roman government. They usually charged more than the person owed in order to stuff their own pockets, and Rome's coffers, hence they became wealthy and were not liked by their own Jewish people.

Matthew, formerly called Levi, collected taxes near the Sea of Galilee. Jesus asked Matthew to follow him as one of His twelve disciples and Matthew did not hesitate. First, he took Jesus to his wealthy home for a feast and invited all his Jewish publican friends to meet Jesus. He wanted them to know that Jesus was the Promised Messiah of the Jews.

When Matthew met Jesus his life changed. He followed Jesus with the twelve for the next three years. After Jesus went back to Heaven, Matthew wrote the *Gospel of Matthew*. He wrote especially to the Jews showing Jesus as their prophesied Messiah and king from David's line. (Matthew 1:1) Other records indicate Matthew may have gone to Parthia and Ethiopia to preach the gospel and may have died as a martyr in A.D. 60. [2]

Zacchaeus, a Jew of Jericho, was another chief publican tax collector for Rome. He was small in stature, hated by the Jews, a rich sinner, and a bit of an outcast because of his job. When Jesus came through Jericho, Zacchaeus wanted to see him, so he climbed up in a tree. Jesus came near and told him to come down because he was going to his house. Joyfully Zacchaeus came to know Jesus and became a changed man. He said if he took any money that didn't belong to him he would pay it back fourfold (Luke 19:8, 9). His so-called Jewish friends became critical, but Jesus told them He came to seek and save those who were sinners. That included Zacchaeus, as well as each and every one of them.

Thought questions:

1. In the story about the Frogs, find an important Root word which appears 12 times with different changes . Change.
changed

---

[2] Foxe, John. *Book of Martyrs*. Barbour, 1989. P. 7 on "Matthew"

2. This word also shows what happened in the lives of the two Bible men mentioned above. This word should also tell what happens in our lives when we came to know Jesus as our Savior. We constantly _Change_ to be more like Him.

3. Is any person too great a sinner that God can not forgive him/her? _no_

4. Can you name some Bible stories which use the number twelve? _Jesus is on the boat with the 12 desicples._

Eggs

Common Toad

Toads and How They Differ from Frogs

On the other hand, **toads** usually live on land and only go to shallow water to lay their masses of eggs. Toad tadpoles are usually black and smaller, but grow into adults in the same way as frogs. One exception is that the toad leaves the water to live on land until the time to lay eggs again.

Toads, which eat insect pests, cutworms, and slugs, are one of the most useful friends of farmers and gardeners. With his long two-inch sticky tongue, the toad captures his prey. Most of the time toads do their helpful work at night and hide under leaves and plants in the day. Toads are never harmful to people, but daily help to destroy the enemy pests in our gardens. We, as Christians, should try to be diligent and useful workers whenever and wherever God places us. The sticky tongue can be a useful instrument in God's hands.

The Stinging Beauty

The jellyfish, a sea animal whose size ranges from pea size to seven feet in diameter, resembles an umbrella or bell. Its name describes the body made up of layers of jelly. They have no spine or bones like other fish. Their color can be orange, pink, blue, or other colors. Tentacles hang down on the edges of the body and trail beneath it. The mouth hangs down from the center like a bell clapper.

Jellyfish swim up by expanding, contracting motions. When the movement stops, the jellyfish floats to the bottom catching other small sea animals for food as it descends. The tentacles contain stinging cells which drive paralyzing poison into a victim. Then the victim is passed into the mouth and swallowed.

Jellyfish can cause painful stings, dangerous to some people. Even though they vary in size and color, all species cause a stinging effect on swimmers. Unknowing people might be tempted to catch a jellyfish. The painful stinging effect would soon bring a change of mind. One jellyfish is so small it is felt before it is seen—like nettles in one's bathing suit. I remember feeling these when we went swimming in the Indian River in Delaware.

Everyone knows what sin is and that everyone has sinned. Sin has a stinging effect on people. Sin can become toxic and addictive as a person continues participating. Sin's victim can be consumed if sin's power is not broken. That power can only be broken by accepting Jesus as Savior and receiving His deliverance from sin's paralyzing effects.

Arctic jellyfish grow larger than others, up to seven feet in diameter. Off the coast of Newfoundland at night I observed jellies the size of a plate, glowing a beautiful bright orange as they swam in the beam of our flashlight. As the tide receded, some died, leaving an orange mass of jelly-like substance on the stony beaches.

The jellyfish forms a thicker substance which supports the animal's body. When I saw the jelly masses on the Newfoundland beaches showing no bones, I thought how much this is like some people who have no spine in making a wise choice and taking a stand for what is right. God wants us to take a firm stand for what is right and not be as flimsy as a jellyfish.

(This article/puzzle were written by Iris and first published by *Nature Friend —* 2.2003.)

Activity Page:

[Use what you have learned to fill in the acrostic. The letters in the vertical squares (down the center) will tell the story's subject.]

Jellyfish are made of layers of ___Jelly___ substances. They live in the ___Sea___. ___Tentacals___ hang down from their outer edge. They have an umbrella or ___Bell___ shape. The size of a ___Jellyfish___ can be tiny or up to 7 feet in diameter. For ___food___ they eat other smaller animals. Some jellyfish look ___Pink___ in color. They have no ___spine___ (backbone) and it isn't shaped like other ___fish___. It ___swims___ by expanding and contracting its tentacles. ___mouth___ hangs down in the center of the tentacles. They excrete ___Poison___ to paralyze victims. They ___expand___ the body to swim. Jellyfish ___cause___ animals and people causing pain to swimmers.

```
        J e l l y
        S e a
t e n t a c l a s
        B e l l
    J e l l y f i s h
        f o o d
        P i n k
        s p i n e
    f i s h
        s w i m s
    m o u t h
        P o i s i n
    e x p a n d
    c a u s e
```

81

House Spider

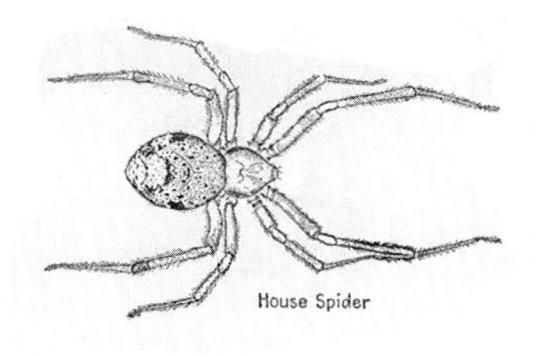

The Spider's Parlor

Once I opened the window and on the window sill I thought I saw a cocoon. I looked at it more closely and observed it looked like a grasshopper wrapped up in a blanket. No, it was a grasshopper wrapped in silk threads. I thought the grasshopper must have accidently gotten in a spider's web, but how could he be wrapped so neatly? I later found when an insect got in a web it was not wrapped, but was held there by a sticky substance.

That friendly spider used his spinnerets to make silk thread which he tightly wrapped around and around the grasshopper so he couldn't move his legs or wings. The poor grasshopper could not escape and would finally die and be stored for the spider's dinner.

There are many species of spiders, or arachnids, meaning they have eight legs and three sections to their bodies and no spinal bones. Most spiders have spinnerets and can spin webs. Spinnerets are short, fingerlike organs attached to the rear of the abdomen, with which the spider spins silk. The silk hardens into thread. Now I know what happened to the grasshopper—he was wrapped up like a mummy in silk thread.

Each species of spider spins his own kind of web, or trap in which he catches his prey or food for dinner. Some are shaped like a lace doily, others like web nests inside of folded leaves, some look like funnels, some very sticky traps, or holes in the ground. These are only a few of the sticky webs made by tricky spiders which form a snare so its victim cannot escape.

Most people are afraid of spiders, but they usually don't bite unless they are threatened and need to protect themselves; however, some spider bites can be harmful to humans. Spiders are really friends because they eat many pests and insects which are harmful to humans—those that bite when they are not provoked, such as mosquitoes, flies, locusts grasshoppers, etc.

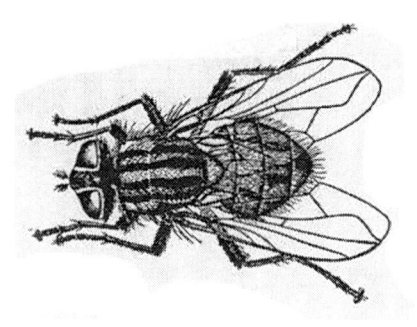

There is a fable "The Spider and the Fly" by Mary Howitt [1]. Find/read the fable on the internet. The fable tells how the spider works to lure its prey. This also reminds us of Satan and the way he sets snares to get the Christian away from God, even to the point of wrapping him up in a bed of sin and leading him to the place of destruction.

1. Note that Satan tells us partial truths as he did with Adam and Eve in the Garden of Eden. He tries to tell us God doesn't mean what he says. Satan stretches the truth and causes our minds to doubt God's words. (Genesis 3)

2. Satan tempts the Christian when he is the weakest and most vulnerable. He promises to give us great things, but doesn't keep his promises. He sets a trap. (Matthew 4:1-10)

3. Satan appeals to our vanity and pride as the spider did with the fly. He flatters us and tells us how pretty we are, how bright we are, and how wise we are, causing our vanity to lead us to the paths of destruction. (Ephesians 6:10-17. Remember the story of King Saul)

4. The fly knew what was in the spider's house. Look at the times he mentions what would happen if he entered the spider's parlor. Sadly enough his vanity got the best of him and he got too close to the wrong place—the spider caught him and destroyed him.

5. Satan blinds people as to the real consequences of giving in to Satan's temptations.

6. Think about the final words of caution from the fable: "The Spider and the Fly" [1]

> *"And now, dear little children, who may this story read,*
> *To idle, silly, flattering words, I pray you never give heed;*
> *Unto an evil counselor close heart, and ear, and eye,*
> *And take a lesson from this tale of the Spider and the Fly."*

Puzzle Question: What lesson can we learn from the Spider and the Fly?

_____
_____
_____
_____
_____

---

[1] Howitt, Mary, "The Spider and the Fly," *101 Famous Poems,* The Cable Company, page 145.

Hold On to God's Truths

Snap! Another insect got caught in the plant's mouth!

A plant with a mouth! Yes, the Venus's-Flytrap has a trap-like mouth. It is a carnivorous plant found in the bogs of North and South America. Because bogs lack nitrogen, God created the plant to catch insects to supply this missing nutrient.

This insect-eating plant grows a foot high, with clusters of white blossoms at the top. The surface of each leaf has three sensitive hairs. The leaf's edge is fringed with sharp bristles. These act as triggers to make the trap work. When an insect touches them, the trap snaps shut. As the victim struggles within, the plant produces digestive juices. The plant's leaves stay closed for a few days until digestion is complete. Then the trap opens to catch its next victim. Here's an odd fact: the plant withers and dies after catching several insects.

This touchy plant lives best in damp areas, but, like other plants, also needs sun as its primary source of energy. The sun produces chlorophyll to carry on photosynthesis.

The Venus's-Flytrap is very sensitive and ready to catch its prey. We as Christians need to be sensitive to God's message. We must catch hold of God's truths and digest them to supply spiritual nutrients which help us grow in Christ. Jesus Christ is also the light of the world. We need to let His light shine through us to show others our source of real life and growth. People need to see in us that He is everything they need each day of their life and for all eternity.

This plant is always ready and waiting for an insect to touch the sensitive hairs at the edge of the leaves. We as Christians should be ready and waiting for any opportunity to serve the Lord. Sometimes we think that preachers, teachers, and missionaries are the only ones serving the Lord. God looks at any type of service for Him as important (2 Corinthians 10:17, 18). However, God sees those who help the preachers and missionaries as equally important in His work. Jesus told his disciples when he washed their feet that he came not to be served, but to serve. He demonstrated this to them when he washed their feet (John 13:14-17).

(First 5 paragraphs were written by Iris and published in *Nature Friend Mag.*, April.2002. and *Seed of Truth*, 2003.)

The Tent—A Temporary Home

(Based on a Personal experience in Newfoundland)

When I camped at a campground in Newfoundland called "Blow-Me-Down" Camp Ground, I had no idea what that name meant until I watched our tent be lifted by a gust of wind and blown toward the Gulf of St. Lawrence. Fortunately the tent got stopped by a row of trees. Everything in the tent was tossed around and got mixed up. Even though modern camping tents are made better than the nomads in Abram's day, they still blow down. I learned firsthand that a tent is not a stable home, but only a temporary moveable house that can be blown down in a moment.

In Abram's day people lived in tents because they could fold them up, more easily and take their flocks and herds to better grass and water. The sheep and cattle needed the grass and water to grow and live. Abram and his family needed the animals and water for food so they could grow and live. Abram knew the tent was his temporary home for the time he spent here on this earth. I'm sure he felt how unstable the tent was sometimes, because it wasn't a strong steady house that could stand against storms and strong wind gusts. Because of what could happen to his tent Abram realized what God meant when He said, "Don't be afraid, I am your shield and your great reward. (Genesis 15:1)

Abram trusted God for a good place to set up his tent, as well as to get water for himself and his animals. God blessed Abram for trusting in His ability to supply the daily needs. Abram knew that he would have a stronger home in Heaven, one that wouldn't blow down or have to be moved from place to place in search of water. He knew the Living Water (Jesus) would be in Heaven and he would never be thirsty again.

Like Abram I need to keep my eyes on the Lord and His strength each day. When we least expect it the stormy gust can blow our tent away. I need to hold on to the truth that "God is my Shield and my Reward" just as He was to Abram. We have a great hope that in Heaven we can look forward to a permanent stable home—a tabernacle not made with man's hands—one that will not blow away. (See 2 Corinthians 5:1)

How can I be sure I'm going to Heaven?
(Use the code below to find the answer.)

The blind man in John 9 was physically and spiritually blind at birth. All people are born spiritually blind, meaning they are sinners from birth. As they get older, they learn right from wrong and know what sin is. These sentences tell what we must do in order to gain our spiritual sight and know we are going to Heaven:

- I must __ __ __ __ __ I am a sinner. (Romans 3:23)
  (1-4-11-9-16)

- I must believe God __ __ __ __ __ me and sent His only
  (10-13-17-15-4)
  Son to die for me. (John 3:16)

- I must __ __ __ __ __ __ __ Jesus died on the cross, where
  (2-5-10-9-5-17-5)
  He took my punishment for sin. (I John 4:14, 15)

- I must _ _ _ _ _ _ _ my sin to God. (Romans 10:9)
  3-13-12-6-5-15-15

Code:
A	B	C	D	E	F	G	H	I	L	M	N	O	R	S	T	V
1	2	3	4	5	6	7	8	9	10	11	12	13	14	15	16	17

Answers for the Puzzle Question Pages

Planets Puzzle (page 15): The eight planets in order are Mercury, Venus, Earth, Mars, Jupiter, Saturn, Uranus, and Neptune

Columbus Puzzle (page 19): Native Americans, year =1492

Sheep Story (page 22): Three chapters in the Bible about the Shepherd and Sheep are Psalms 23, Isaiah 53 and John 10. Isaiah 40:11 "He shall feed His flock like a Shepherd: He shall gather the lambs with His arms, and carry them in His bosom, and shall gently lead those that are with young."

Chimp Puzzle (page 24): God told a great man in the Bible to ask for anything he wanted and God would give it. (I Kings 3:5, 9-12) Who was this man? Solomon . What did he ask for? wisdom. Was God pleased with his choice? _Yes. Did God give him his wish? Yes

Dog Puzzle (page30): friends, friend. Proverbs 18:24 . Jesus wants to be that friend to you.

Wolf Puzzle: (page 32):
xanxxxexamplexxxfromxxnaturexxthexxxxwolfxhasxaxxfamilyxinxxdensx
    (Answer: An example from nature—The wolf has a family in dens)

Groundhog Puzzle (page 38): Jeremiah 17:7. Fill in the blanks: Trusts, LORD.

Lion Puzzle (page 46): From Daniel 6:10, Daniel prayed 3 times a day. The lions were hungry, but God closed their mouths in verse 22. They were hungry in verse 24.

Life in Darkness Puzzle (page 48): 1. Jesus, the Light of the World. 2."Amazing grace, how sweet the sound, that saved a wretch like me; I once was lost but now am found, was blind, but now I see."

Getting Attention Puzzle (page 68): Mark 1:6—John the Baptist ate locusts and wild honey.

Tadpole Puzzle (page 77, 78): 1. The Root Word that appears 12 times in the story is Change. 2. Change 3. No. 4. Twelve appears in the Bible for the 12 tribes of Israel or 12 sons of Jacob; 12 disciples; 12 gates on the Heavenly city with 12 angels, one at each gate in Revelation 21.

Jellyfish Puzzle (page 81):
    [Use what you have learned to fill in the acrostic. The letters in the vertical squares (down the center) will tell the story's subject.]

Answers: Jelly, sea, tentacles, bell, jellyfish, food, pink, spine, fish, swim, mouth, poison, expand, sting. Vertical Answer is: jellyfish sting

"Spider and Fly" Puzzle (page 84): When we know what is right we need to be careful not to get trapped by flattering words. We should learn not to be controlled by our vanity.

The Tent–Heaven Puzzle (page 88): Admit, loved, believe, confess.

Challenges from the Author

It is my desire that you will grow spiritually from reading these stories.

God designed His creation to grow physically, but he has blessed humans with body, soul, and spirit. This affords humans the opportunity to not only grow physically, but mentally, emotionally, and spiritually.

This page is for the reader's reactions, corrections, and comments. Please use this e-mail address to send your comments to the author: irisgdow@juno.com or irisgdow@zoominternet.com — Please include your name, address, phone, and e-mail. If you do not receive a reply contact: info@FaithfulLifePublishers.com

Perhaps you have been inspired by these stories and would like to write one of your own. Why don't you try it? When you are finished send the story to the email address above and I will help you prepare it for publication. I'll keep a folder of stories for the next book. It may take a few years to collect enough for another book, but have patience. Meanwhile, you will be free to use your story in any way you wish. Your story will carry you name. There will be no money or payment involved since I would take care of the publishing costs.

Here are some other books written by Iris Gray Dowling. Contact her by e-mail.

- History of Churches and Worship Groups in the Oxford Area. (176 pages)
- A Change of Hats—Picture Book for Kindergarten age.
- A Pony for my Birthday—Easy Reader for Grades 1 to 3.
- Mission Journeys from Upper Oxford Township
- School and Church Program Ideas for the Whole Year
- Christmas Program Ideas
- Upward Bound (puppet skits)
- Declare His Name (mission dramas for mission conferences)
- Through the Eye-Gate (object lessons)

Brief Bio of the Author

Iris Gray Dowling has been active in Elementary education for over 50 years (25+ in public schools, 23+ as homeschool advisor, 45 years as a Junior Church teacher, as well as Vacation Bible School and Sunday school). She enjoys getting children involved in studying God's magnificent creation.

Iris has been a freelance writer for nearly 50 years. As a result of her study and teaching it is her desire that her readers will realize that God's creation far exceeds anything man can do and that nothing was created by chance—only by the mastermind of God.

The author hopes to motivate families to read and investigate more of God's creative genius and maintain an open mind to see God's eternal plan for each person He created.